THE CIVIL WAR
IN FRANCE: THE
PARIS COMMUNE

KARL MARX AND V. I. LENIN

THE CIVIL WAR
IN FRANCE: THE
PARIS COMMUNE

2nd Edition

*The complete edition of Marx's
three addresses on the Franco-Prussian
War of 1870-71 and the Commune, and
Lenin's writings on the Commune
with Nikita Fedorovsky's
"Marx's 'Civil War in France' "
as a Supplementary essay*

INTERNATIONAL PUBLISHERS

New York

Library of Congress Cataloging-in-Publication Data

The Civil War in France

    The complete edition of Marx's three addresses on the Franco-Prussian War of 1870-71 and the Commune, Lenin's Writings on the Commune, with Nikita Fedorovsky's "Marx's 'Civil War in France' " as a supplementary essay.
    1. Paris (France)—History—Commune, 1871. I. Marx, Karl, 1818-1883. Burgerkrieg in Frankreich. English. 1988. II. Lenin, Vladimir Il'ich, 1870-1924. Selections. English. 1988. III. Fedorovsky, Nikita. Marx's Civil War in France. 1988.
DC317.C58 1988   944.081'2   88-24454
ISBN10: 0-7178-0666-9
ISBN13: 978-0-7178-0666-9

© International Publisher Co., Inc.
1940, 1968, 1988.

Fedorovsky text by arrangement with
Progress Publishers, Moscow   © 1985

This printing, 2016

EDITOR'S NOTE

Here is gathered in a single volume the full text of *The Civil War in France* by Karl Marx, with Frederick Engels' Introduction to the German edition of 1891, comprising Part I, V. I. Lenin's writings on the Paris Commune as Part II, and Nikita Fedorovsky's essay, "Marx's 'Civil War in France' " as a supplementary essay, Part III.

Following Engels' suggestion in his Introduction, written on the twentieth anniversary of the Commune, the two shorter Addresses on the Franco-Prussian War are included ahead of the celebrated Address in which Marx drew the classic lessons of the rise and fall of the Commune. All three Addresses are printed according to the English text as published at the time by the General Council of the International Working Men's Association. (The first two Addresses were printed in leaflet form in English, German and French, and the third as pamphlets in the same languages.) The Notes immediately following the third Address were included in the English pamphlet of 1871. The editor has added, to complete Part I, excerpts from two letters to Dr. Kugelmann, in which Marx makes several significant observations on the Commune.

Most of Lenin's writings which appear, in chronological order, in Part II of the present volume had been previously published in *The Paris Commune* (International Publishers, 1934). They are now published in new and revised translation, based on the latest edition of Lenin's *Collected Works* (Progress Publishers, Moscow). Included is the chapter from *State and Revolution* dealing with the experiences of the Commune, for here the importance that Lenin attributed to Marx's estimate can best be seen in the context of Lenin's own theoretical conclusions on the state. Subsequent writings included in Part II reflect Lenin's view that the young Soviet Republic stood on the shoulders of the Paris Commune.

The editor has supplied explanatory notes, pp. 133-142, numbered consecutively for each Part separately.

CONTENTS

CONTENTS

PART ONE

THE CIVIL WAR IN FRANCE
by Karl Marx

INTRODUCTION

by FREDERICK ENGELS

I DID not anticipate that I would be asked to prepare a new edition of the Address of the General Council of the International on *The Civil War in France,* and to write an introduction to it. Therefore I can only touch briefly here on the most important points.

I am prefacing the longer work mentioned above by the two shorter Addresses of the General Council on the Franco-Prussian War. In the first place, because the second of these, which itself cannot be fully understood without the first, is referred to in *The Civil War.* But also because these two Addresses, likewise drafted by Marx, are, no less than *The Civil War,* outstanding examples of the author's remarkable gift, first proved in *The Eighteenth Brumaire of Louis Bonaparte,* for grasping clearly the character, the import, and the necessary consequences of great historical events, at a time when these events are still in process before our eyes, or have only just taken place. And, finally, because we in Germany are still having to endure the consequences which Marx prophesied would follow from these events.

Has that which was declared in the first Address not come to pass: that if Germany's defensive war against Louis Bonaparte degenerated into a war of conquest against the French people, all the misfortunes which befell Germany after the so-called wars of liberation [1] would revive again with renewed intensity? Have we not had a further twenty years of Bismarck's government, the Exceptional Law and the anti-socialist campaign taking the place of the prosecutions of "demagogues," with the same arbitrary police measures and with literally the same staggering interpretations of the law?

And has not the prophecy been proved to the letter that the

annexation of Alsace-Lorraine would "force France into the arms
of Russia,"² and that after this annexation Germany must either
become the avowed tool of Russia, or must, after some short respite,
arm for a new war, and, moreover, "a war with the combined
Slavonian and Roman races"? Has not the annexation of the French
provinces driven France into the arms of Russia? Has not Bismarck
for fully twenty years vainly wooed the favour of the tsar, wooed
it with services even more lowly than those which little Prussia,
before it became the "first Power in Europe," was wont to lay at
Holy Russia's feet? And is there not every day hanging over our
heads the Damocles' sword of war, on the first day of which all the
chartered covenants of princes will be scattered like chaff; a war
of which nothing is certain but the absolute uncertainty of its outcome; a race war which will subject the whole of Europe to devas-
tation by fifteen or twenty million armed men, and is only not
already raging because even the strongest of the great military states
shrinks before the absolute incalculability of its final outcome?

All the more is it our duty to make again accessible to the German
workers these brilliant proofs, now half-forgotten, of the far-sighted-
ness of international working class policy in 1870.

What is true of these two Addresses is also true of *The Civil
War in France*. On May 28, the last fighters of the Commune suc-
cumbed to superior forces on the slopes of Belleville; and only two
days later, on May 30, Marx read to the General Council the work
in which the historical significance of the Paris Commune is de-
lineated in short powerful strokes, but with such clearness, and
above all such truth, as has never again been attained in all the mass
of literature which has been written on this subject.

Thanks to the economic and political development of France since
1789, for fifty years the position in Paris has been such that no
revolution could break out there without assuming a proletarian
character, that is to say, without the proletariat, which had bought
victory with its blood, advancing its own demands after victory.
These demands were more or less unclear and even confused, corresponding to the state of evolution reached by the workers of Paris
at the particular period, but in the last resort they all amounted

to the abolition of the class antagonism between capitalists and workers. It is true that no one knew how this was to be brought about. But the demand itself, however indefinite it still was in its formulation, contained a threat to the existing order of society; the workers who put it forward were still armed; therefore the disarming of the workers was the first commandment for the bourgeois at the helm of the state. Hence, after every revolution won by the workers, a new struggle, ending with the defeat of the workers.

This happened for the first time in 1848. The liberal bourgeoisie of the parliamentary opposition held banquets for securing reform of the franchise, which was to ensure supremacy for their party. Forced more and more, in their struggle with the government, to appeal to the people, they had to allow the radical and republican strata of the bourgeoisie and petty bourgeoisie gradually to take the lead. But behind these stood the revolutionary workers, and since 1830 these had acquired far more political independence than the bourgeoisie, and even the republicans, suspected. At the moment of the crisis between the government and the opposition, the workers opened battle on the streets; Louis Philippe vanished, and with him the franchise reform; and in its place arose the republic, and indeed one which the victorious workers themselves designated as a "social" republic. No one, however, was clear as to what this social republic was to imply; not even the workers themselves. But they now had arms in their hands, and were a power in the state. Therefore, as soon as the bourgeois republicans in control felt something like firm ground under their feet, their first aim was to disarm the workers. This took place by driving them into the insurrection of June 1848 by direct breach of faith, by open defiance and the attempt to banish the unemployed to a distant province. The government had taken care to have an overwhelming superiority of force. After five days' heroic struggle, the workers were defeated. And then followed a blood-bath of the defenceless prisoners, the like of which has not been seen since the days of the civil wars which ushered in the downfall of the Roman republic. It was the first time that the bourgeoisie showed to what insane cruelties of revenge they will be goaded the moment the proletariat dares to takes its stand against them as a separate class, with its own interests and demands. And yet 1848 was only child's play compared with their frenzy in 1871.

Punishment followed hard at heel. If the proletariat was not yet able to rule France, the bourgeoisie could no longer do so. At least not at that period, when the greater part of it was still monarchically inclined, and it was divided into three dynastic parties [3] and a fourth republican party. Its internal dissensions allowed the adventurer Louis Bonaparte to take possession of all the commanding points—army, police, administrative machinery—and, on December 2, 1851,[4] to explode the last stronghold of the bourgeoisie, the National Assembly. The Second Empire [5] opened the exploitation of France by a gang of political and financial adventurers, but at the same time also an industrial development such as had never been possible under the narrow-minded and timorous system of Louis Philippe, with its exclusive domination by only a small section of the big bourgeoisie. Louis Bonaparte took the political power from the capitalists under the pretext of protecting them, the bourgeoisie, from the workers, and on the other hand the workers from them; but in return his rule encouraged speculation and industrial activity—in a word the rise and enrichment of the whole bourgeoisie to an extent hitherto unknown. To an even greater extent, it is true, corruption and mass robbery developed, clustering around the imperial court, and drawing their heavy percentages from this enrichment.

But the Second Empire was the appeal to French chauvinism, the demand for the restoration of the frontiers of the First Empire, which had been lost in 1814, or at least those of the First Republic. A French empire within the frontiers of the old monarchy and, in fact, within the even more amputated frontiers of 1815—such a thing was impossible for any long duration of time. Hence the necessity for brief wars and extension of frontiers. But no extension of frontiers was so dazzling to the imagination of the French chauvinists as the extension to the German left bank of the Rhine. One square mile on the Rhine was more to them than ten in the Alps or anywhere else. Given the Second Empire, the demand for the restoration to France of the left bank of the Rhine, either all at once or piecemeal, was merely a question of time. The time came with the Austro-Prussian War of 1866;[6] cheated of the anticipated "territorial compensation" by Bismarck and by his own over-cunning, hesitating policy, there was now nothing left for Napoleon but war, which broke out in 1870 and drove him first to Sedan,[7] and thence to Wilhelmshöhe.

The inevitable result was the Paris Revolution of September 4, 1870. The empire collapsed like a house of cards, and the republic was again proclaimed. But the enemy was standing at the gates; the armies of the empire were either hopelessly beleaguered in Metz or held captive in Germany. In this emergency the people allowed the Paris deputies to the former legislative body to constitute themselves into a "Government of National Defence." This was the more readily conceded, since, for the purposes of defence, all Parisians capable of bearing arms had enrolled in the National Guard and were armed, so that now the workers constituted a great majority. But almost at once the antagonism between the almost completely bourgeois government and the armed proletariat broke into open conflict. On October 31, workers' battalions stormed the town hall, and captured some members of the government. Treachery, the government's direct breach of its undertakings, and the intervention of some petty-bourgeois battalions set them free again, and in order not to occasion the outbreak of civil war inside a city which was already beleaguered by a foreign power, the former government was left in office.

At last, on January 8, 1871, Paris, almost starving, capitulated but with honours unprecedented in the history of war. The forts were surrendered, the outer wall disarmed, the weapons of the regiments of the line and of the Mobile Guard [8] were handed over, and they themselves considered prisoners of war. But the National Guard kept its weapons and guns, and only entered into an armistice with the victors, who themselves did not dare enter Paris in triumph. They only dared to occupy a tiny corner of Paris, which, into the bargain, consisted partly of public parks, and even this they only occupied for a few days! And during this time they, who had maintained their encirclement of Paris for 131 days, were themselves encircled by the armed workers of Paris, who kept a sharp watch that no "Prussian" should overstep the narrow bounds of the corner ceded to the foreign conquerors. Such was the respect which the Paris workers inspired in the army before which all the armies of the empire had laid down their arms; and the Prussian *Junkers,* who had come to take revenge at the very centre of the revolution, were compelled to stand by respectfully, and salute just precisely this armed revolution!

During the war the Paris workers had confined themselves to demanding the vigorous prosecution of the fight. But now, when peace had come after the capitulation of Paris, now, Thiers, the new head of the government, was compelled to realise that the supremacy of the propertied classes—large landowners and capitalists— was in constant danger so long as the workers of Paris had arms in their hands. His first action was to attempt to disarm them. On March 18, he sent troops of the line with orders to rob the National Guard of the artillery belonging to it, which had been constructed during the siege of Paris and had been paid for by subscription. The attempt failed; Paris mobilised as one man in defence of the guns, and war between Paris and the French government sitting at Versailles was declared. On March 26 the Paris Commune was elected and on March 28 it was proclaimed. The Central Committee of the National Guard, which up to then had carried on the government, handed in its resignation to the National Guard, after it had first decreed the abolition of the scandalous Paris "Morality Police." On March 30 the Commune abolished conscription and the standing army, and declared that the National Guard, in which all citizens capable of bearing arms were to be enrolled, was to be the sole armed force. It remitted all payments of rent for dwelling houses from October 1870 until April, the amounts already paid to be reckoned to a future rental period, and stopped all sales of articles pledged in the municipal pawnshops. On the same day the foreigners elected to the Commune were confirmed in office, because "the flag of the Commune is the flag of the World Republic."

On April 1 it was decided that the highest salary received by any employee of the Commune, and therefore also by its members themselves, might not exceed 6,000 francs. On the following day the Commune decreed the separation of the Church from the State, and the abolition of all state payments for religious purposes as well as the transformation of all Church property into national property; as a result of which, on April 8, a decree excluding from the schools all religious symbols, pictures, dogmas, prayers—in a word, "all that belongs to the sphere of the individual's conscience" —was ordered to be excluded from the schools, and this decree was gradually applied. On the 5th, in reply to the shooting, day after day, of the Commune's fighters captured by the Versailles troops, a decree was issued for imprisonment of hostages, but it was never carried into effect. On the 6th, the guillotine was brought out by the 137th battalion of the National Guard, and publicly burnt, amid great popular rejoicing. On the 12th, the Commune decided that the Victory Column on the Place Vendôme, which had been cast from guns captured by Napoleon after the war of 1809, should be demolished as a symbol of chauvinism and incitement to national hatred. This decree was carried out on May 16. On April 16 the Commune ordered a statistical tabulation of factories which had been closed down by the manufacturers, and the working out of plans for the carrying on of these factories by workers formerly employed in them, who were to be organised in co-operative societies, and also plans for the organisation of these co-operatives in one great union. On the 20th the Commune abolished night work for bakers, and also the workers' registration cards, which since the Second Empire had been run as a monopoly by police nominees— exploiters of the first rank; the issuing of these registration cards was transferred to the mayors[9] of the twenty *arrondissements* of Paris. On April 30 the Commune ordered the closing of the pawnshops, on the ground that they were a private exploitation of labour, and were in contradiction with the right of the workers to their instruments of labour and to credit. On May 5 it ordered the demolition of the Chapel of Atonement, which had been built in expiation of the execution of Louis XVI.[10]

Thus, from March 18 onwards the class character of the Paris movement, which had previously been pushed into the background by the fight against the foreign invaders, emerged sharply and clearly. As almost without exception, workers, or recognised representatives of the workers, sat in the Commune, its decisions bore a decidedly proletarian character. Either they decreed reforms which the republican bourgeoisie had failed to pass solely out of cowardice, but which provided a necessary basis for the free activity of the working class—such as the realisation of the principle that *in relation to the state*, religion is a purely private matter—or they promulgated decrees which were in the direct interests of the working class and to some extent cut deeply into the old order of society. In a beleaguered city, however, it was possible at most to make a start in the realisation of all these measures. And from the beginning of May onwards all their energies were taken up by the fight against the ever-growing armies assembled by the Versailles government.

On April 7 the Versailles troops had captured the Seine crossing at Neuilly, on the western front of Paris; on the other hand, in an attack on the southern front on the 11th they were repulsed with heavy losses by General Eudes. Paris was continually bombarded and, moreover, by the very people who had stigmatised as a sacrilege the bombardment of the same city by the Prussians. These same people now begged the Prussian government for the hasty return of the French soldiers taken prisoner at Sedan and Metz, in order that they might recapture Paris for them. From the beginning of May the gradual arrival of these troops gave the Versailles forces a decided ascendancy. This already became evident when, on April 23, Thiers broke off the negotiations for the exchange, proposed by the Commune, of the Archbishop of Paris and a whole number of other priests held as hostages in Paris, for only one man, Blanqui, who had twice been elected to the Commune but was a prisoner in Clairvaux. And even more in the changed language of Thiers; previously procrastinating and equivocal, he now suddenly became insolent, threatening, brutal. The Versailles forces took the redoubt of Moulin Saquet on the southern front, on May 3; on the 9th, Fort Issy, which had been completely reduced to ruins by gunfire; and on the 14th, Fort Vanves. On the western front they advanced gradually, capturing the numerous villages and buildings which extended up to the city wall, until they reached the main wall itself; on the 21st, thanks to treachery and the carelessness of the National Guards stationed there, they succeeded in forcing their way into the city. The Prussians who held the northern and eastern forts allowed the Versailles troops to advance across the land north of the city, which was forbidden ground to them under the armistice, and thus to march forward and attack on a long front, which the Parisians naturally thought covered by the armistice, and therefore held only with weak forces. As a result of this, only a weak resistance was put up in the western half of Paris, in the luxury city proper; it grew stronger and more tenacious the nearer the incoming troops approached the eastern half, the real working class city.

It was only after eight days' fighting that the last defenders of the Commune were overwhelmed on the heights of Belleville and Menilmontant; and then the massacre of defenceless men, women and children, which had been raging all through the week on an increasing scale, reached its zenith. The breechloaders could no longer kill fast enough; the vanquished workers were shot down in hundreds by mitrailleuse fire. The "Wall of the Federals" at the Père Lachaise cemetery, where the final mass murder was consummated, is still standing today, a mute but eloquent testimony to the savagery of which the ruling class is capable as soon as the working class dares to come out for its rights. Then came the mass arrests; when the slaughter of them all proved to be impossible, the shooting of victims arbitrarily selected from the prisoners' ranks, and the removal of the rest to great camps where they awaited trial by courts-martial. The Prussian troops surrounding the northern half of Paris had orders not to allow any fugitives to pass; but the officers often shut their eyes when the soldiers paid more obedience to the dictates of humanity than to those of the General Staff; particularly, honour is due to the Saxon army corps, which behaved very humanely and let through many workers who were obviously fighters for the Commune.

If today, after twenty years, we look back at the activity and historical significance of the Paris Commune of 1871, we shall find it necessary to make a few additions to the account given in *The Civil War in France.*

The members of the Commune were divided into a majority, the Blanquists, who had also been predominant in the Central Committee of the National Guard; and a minority, members of the International Working Men's Association, chiefly consisting of adherents of the Proudhon school of socialism. The great majority of the Blanquists at that time were socialists only by revolutionary and proletarian instinct; only a few had attained greater clarity on the essential principles, through Vaillant, who was familiar with German scientific socialism. It is therefore comprehensible that in the economic sphere much was left undone which, according to our view today, the Commune ought to have done. The hardest thing to understand is certainly the holy awe with which they remained standing respectfully outside the gates of the Bank of France. This was also a serious political mistake. The bank in the hands of the Commune—this would have been worth more than ten thousand hostages. It would have meant the pressure of the whole of the French bourgeoisie on the Versailles government in favour of peace with the Commune. But what is still more wonderful is the correctness of so much that was actually done by the Commune, composed as it was of Blanquists and Proudhonists. Naturally, the Proudhonists were chiefly responsible for the economic decrees of the Commune, both for their praiseworthy and their unpraiseworthy aspects; as the Blanquists were for its political actions and omissions. And in both cases the irony of history willed—as is usual when doctrinaires come to the helm— that both did the opposite of what the doctrines of their school prescribed.

Proudhon, the Socialist of the small peasant and master-craftsman, regarded association with positive hatred. He said of it that there was more bad than good in it; that it was by nature sterile, even harmful, because it was a fetter on the freedom of the workers; that it was a pure dogma, unproductive and burdensome, in conflict as much with the freedom of the workers as with economy of labour; that its disadvantages multiplied more swiftly than its advantages; that, as compared with it, competition, division of labour and private property were economic forces. Only for the exceptional cases—as Proudhon called them—of large-scale industry and large industrial units, such as railways, was there any place for the association of workers. (*Cf. Idée Générale de la Révolution, 3 étude.*)

By 1871, even in Paris, the centre of handicrafts, large-scale industry had already so much ceased to be an exceptional case that by far the most important decree of the Commune instituted an organisation of large-scale industry and even of manufacture which was not based only on the association of workers in each factory, but also aimed at combining all these associations in one great union; in short an organisation which, as Marx quite rightly says in *The Civil War*, must necessarily have led in the end to communism, that is to say, the direct antithesis of the Proudhon doctrine. And, therefore, the Commune was also the grave of the Proudhon school of socialism. Today this school has vanished from French working class circles; among them now, among the Possibilists [11] no less than among the "Marxists," Marx's theory rules unchallenged. Only among the "radical" bourgeoisie are there still Proudhonists.

The Blanquists fared no better. Brought up in the school of conspiracy, and held together by the strict discipline which went with it, they started out from the viewpoint that a relatively small number of resolute, well-organised men would be able, at a given favourable moment, not only to seize the helm of state, but also by energetic and relentless action, to keep power until they succeeded in drawing the mass of the people into the revolution and ranging them round the small band of leaders. This conception involved, above all, the strictest dictatorship, and centralisation of all power in the hands of the new revolutionary government. And what did the Commune, with its majority of these same Blanquists, actually do? In all its proclamations to the French in the provinces, it proposed to them a free federation of all French Communes with Paris, a national organisation, which for the first time was really to be created by the nation itself. It was precisely the oppressing power of the former centralised government, army, political police and bureaucracy, which Napoleon had created in 1798 and since then had been taken over by every new government as a welcome instrument and used against its opponents, it was precisely this power which was to fall everywhere, just as it had already fallen in Paris.

From the outset the Commune was compelled to recognise that the working class, once come to power, could not manage with the old state machine; that in order not to lose again its only just conquered supremacy, this working class must, on the one hand, do away with all the old repressive machinery previously used against it itself, and, on the other, safeguard itself against its own deputies and officials, by declaring them all, without exception, subject to recall at any moment. What had been the characteristic attribute of the former state? Society had created its own organs to look after its common interests, originally through simple division of labour. But these organs, at whose head was the state power, had in the course of time, in pursuance of their own special interests, transformed themselves from the servants of society into the masters of society, as can be seen, for example, not only in the hereditary monarchy, but equally also in the democratic republic. Nowhere do "politicians" form a more separate, powerful section of the nation than in North America. There, each of the two great parties [12] which alternately succeed each other in power is itself in turn controlled by people who make a business of politics, who speculate on seats in the legislative assemblies of the Union as well as of the separate states, or who make a living by carrying on agitation for their party and on its victory are rewarded with positions.

It is well known that the Americans have been striving for thirty years to shake off this yoke, which has become intolerable, and that in spite of all they can do they continue to sink ever deeper in this swamp of corruption. It is precisely in America that we see best how there takes place this process of the state power making itself independent in relation to society, whose mere instrument it was originally intended to be. Here there exists no dynasty, no nobility, no standing army, beyond the few men keeping watch on the Indians, no bureaucracy with permanent posts or the right to pensions. And nevertheless we find here two great gangs of political speculators, who alternately take possession of the state power and exploit it by the most corrupt means and for the most corrupt ends —and the nation is powerless against these two great cartels of politicians, who are ostensibly its servants, but in reality exploit and plunder it.

Against this transformation of the state and the organs of the state from servants of society into masters of society—an inevitable transformation in all previous states—the Commune made use of two infallible expedients. In the first place, it filled all posts— administrative, judicial and educational—by election on the basis of universal suffrage of all concerned, with the right of the same electors to recall their delegate at any time. And in the second place, all officials, high or low, were paid only the wages received by other workers. The highest salary paid by the Commune to anyone was 6,000 francs. In this way an effective barrier to place-hunting and careerism was set up, even apart from the binding mandates to delegates to representative bodies which were also added in pro- fusion.

This shattering of the former state power and its replacement by a new and really democratic state is described in detail in the third section of *The Civil War*. But it was necessary to dwell briefly here once more on some of its features, because in Germany particularly the superstitious belief in the state has been carried over from philosophy into the general consciousness of the bour- geoisie and even to many workers. According to the philosophical notion, the state is the "realisation of the idea" or the Kingdom of God on earth, translated into philosophical terms, the sphere in which eternal truth and justice is or should be realised. And from this follows a superstitious reverence for the state and everything connected with it, which takes root the more readily as people from their childhood are accustomed to imagine that the affairs and interests common to the whole of society could not be looked after otherwise than as they have been looked after in the past, that is, through the state and its well-paid officials. And people think they have taken quite an extraordinarily bold step forward when they have rid themselves of belief in hereditary monarchy and swear by the democratic republic. In reality, however, the state is nothing but a machine for the oppression of one class by another, and indeed in the democratic republic no less than in the monarchy; and at best an evil inherited by the proletariat after its victorious struggle for class supremacy, whose worst sides the proletariat, just like the Commune, cannot avoid having to lop off at the earliest possible moment, until such time as a new generation, reared in new and free social conditions, will be able to throw the entire lumber of the state on the scrap-heap.

Of late, the Social-Democratic philistine[18] has once more been filled with wholesome terror at the words: Dictatorship of the Proletariat. Well and good, gentlemen, do you want to know what this dictatorship looks like? Look at the Paris Commune. That was the Dictatorship of the Proletariat.

FREDERICK ENGELS

London, on the twentieth anniversary
of the Paris Commune, March 18, 1891.

I

First Address of the General Council on the Franco-Prussian War

To the Members of the International Working Men's Association in Europe and the United States

In the Inaugural Address of the International Working Men's Association, of November 1864, we said: "If the emancipation of the working classes requires their fraternal concurrence, how are they to fulfil that great mission with a foreign policy in pursuit of criminal designs, playing upon national prejudices, and squandering in piratical wars the people's blood and treasure?" We defined the foreign policy aimed at by the International in these words: "Vindicate the simple laws of morals and justice, which ought to govern the relations of private individuals, as the laws paramount of the intercourse of nations."

No wonder that Louis Bonaparte, who usurped his power by exploiting the war of classes in France, and perpetuated it by periodical wars abroad, should, from the first, have treated the International as a dangerous foe. On the eve of the plebiscite [14] he ordered a raid on the members of the Administrative Committees of the International Working Men's Association throughout France, at Paris, Lyons, Rouen, Marseilles, Brest, etc.,[15] on the pretext that the International was a secret society dabbling in a *complot* for his assassination, a pretext soon after exposed in its full absurdity by his own judges. What was the real crime of the French branches of the International? They told the French people publicly and emphatically that voting the plebiscite was voting despotism at home and war abroad. It has been, in fact, their work that in all the great towns, in all the industrial centres of France, the working class rose like one man to reject the plebiscite. Unfortunately the balance was turned by the heavy ignorance of the rural districts. The stock exchanges, the cabinets, the ruling classes and the press of Europe celebrated the plebiscite as a signal victory of the French emperor over the French working class; and it was the signal for the assassination, not of an individual, but of nations.

The war plot of July 1870 [16] is but an amended edition of the *coup d'état* of December 1851. At first view the thing seemed so absurd that France would not believe in its real good earnest. It rather believed the deputy denouncing the ministerial war talk as a mere stock-jobbing trick. When, on July 15, war was at last officially announced to the *Corps Législatif,* the whole Opposition refused to vote the preliminary subsidies—even Thiers branded it as "detestable"; all the independent journals of Paris condemned it, and, wonderful to relate, the provincial press joined in almost unanimously.

Meanwhile, the Paris members of the International had again set to work. In the *Reveil* of July 12 they published their manifesto "to the Workmen of all Nations," from which we extract the following few passages:

"Once more," they say, "on the pretext of European equilibrium, of national honour, the peace of the world is menaced by political ambitions. French, German, Spanish workmen! Let our voices unite in one cry of reprobation against war!... War for a question of preponderance or a dynasty can, in the eyes of workmen, be nothing but a criminal absurdity. In answer to the warlike proclamations of those who exempt themselves from the blood tax, and find in public misfortunes a source of fresh speculations, we protest, we who want peace, labour and liberty!... Brothers in Germany! Our division would only result in the complete triumph of the despotism on both sides of the Rhine.... Workmen of all countries! Whatever may for the present become of our common efforts, we, the members of the International Working Men's Association, who know of no frontiers, we send you, as a pledge of indissoluble solidarity, the good wishes and the salutations of the workmen of France."

This manifesto of our Paris section was followed by numerous similar French addresses, of which we can here only quote the declaration of Neuilly-sur-Seine, published in the *Marseillaise* of July 22:

"The war, is it just? No! The war, is it national? No! It is merely dynastic. In the name of humanity, or democracy, and the true interests of France, we adhere completely and energetically to the protestation of the International against the war."

These protestations expressed the true sentiments of the French working people, as was soon shown by a curious incident. *The Band of the Tenth of December,*[17] first organised under the presidency of Louis Bonaparte, having been masqueraded into *blouses* and let loose on the streets of Paris, there to perform the contortions of war fever, the real workmen of the Faubourgs came forward with public peace demonstrations so overwhelming that Pietri, the Prefect of Police, thought it prudent to stop at once all further street politics, on the plea that the real Paris people had given sufficient vent to their pent-up patriotism and exuberant war enthusiasm.

Whatever may be the incidents of Louis Bonaparte's war with Prussia, the death-knell of the Second Empire has already sounded at Paris. It will end, as it began, by a parody. But let us not forget that it is the governments and the ruling classes of Europe who enabled Louis Bonaparte to play during eighteen years the ferocious farce of the *Restored Empire.*

On the German side, the war is a war of defence;[18] but who put Germany to the necessity of defending herself? Who enabled Louis Bonaparte to wage war upon her? *Prussia!* It was Bismarck who conspired with that very same Louis Bonaparte for the purpose of crushing popular opposition at home, and annexing Germany to the Hohenzollern dynasty. If the battle of Sadowa[19] had been lost instead of being won, French battalions would have overrun Germany as the allies of Prussia. After her victory, did Prussia dream one moment of opposing a free Germany to an enslaved France? Just the contrary. While carefully preserving all the native beauties of her old system, she super-added all the tricks of the Second Empire, its real despotism and its mock democratism, its political shams and its financial jobs, its high-flown talk and its low *legerdemains*. The Bonapartist regime, which till then only flourished on one side of the Rhine, had now got its counterfeit on the other. From such a state of things, what else could result but *war?*

If the German working class allows the present war to lose its strictly defensive character and to degenerate into a war against the French people, victory or defeat will prove alike disastrous. All the miseries that befell Germany after her war of independence will revive with accumulated intensity.

The principles of the International are, however, too widely spread and too firmly rooted amongst the German working class to apprehend such a sad consummation. The voices of the French workmen had re-echoed from Germany. A mass meeting of workmen, held at Brunswick on July 16, expressed its full concurrence with the Paris manifesto, spurned the idea of national antagonism to France, and wound up its resolutions with these words:

"We are enemies of all wars, but above all of dynastic wars.[20] ... With deep sorrow and grief we are forced to undergo a defensive war as an unavoidable evil; but we call, at the same time, upon the whole German working class to render the recurrence of such an immense social misfortune impossible by vindicating for the peoples themselves the power to decide on peace and war, and making them masters of their own destinies."

At Chemnitz, a meeting of delegates, representing 50,000 Saxon workmen, adopted unanimously a resolution to this effect:

"In the name of the German Democracy, and especially of the workmen forming the Democratic Socialist Party, we declare the present war to be exclusively dynastic.... We are happy to grasp the fraternal hand stretched out to us by the workmen of France.... Mindful of the watchword of the International Working Men's Association: *Proletarians of all countries, unite,* we shall never forget that the workmen of *all* countries are our *friends* and the despots of *all* countries our *enemies.*"

The Berlin branch of the International has also replied to the Paris manifesto:

"We," they say, "join with heart and hand your protestation. . . . Solemnly we promise that neither the sound of the trumpet, nor the roar of the cannon, neither victory nor defeat, shall divert us from our common work for the union of the children of toil of all countries."

Be it so!

In the background of this suicidal strike looms the dark figure of Russia. It is an ominous sign that the signal for the present war should have been given at the moment when the Moscovite government had just finished its strategic lines of railway and was already massing troops in the direction of the Pruth. Whatever sympathy the Germans may justly claim in a war of defence against Bonapartist aggression, they would forfeit at once by allowing the Prussian government to call for, or accept the help of, the Cossack. Let them remember that after their war of independence against the first Napoleon, Germany lay for generations prostrate at the feet of the tsar.[21]

The English working class stretch the hand of fellowship to the French and German working people. They feel deeply convinced that whatever turn the impending horrid war may take, the alliance of the working classes of all countries will ultimately kill war. The very fact that while official France and Germany are rushing into a fratricidal feud, the workmen of France and Germany send each other messages of peace and goodwill; this great fact, unparalleled in the history of the past, opens the vista of a brighter future. It proves that in contrast to old society, with its economical miseries and its political delirium, a new society is springing up, whose International rule will be *Peace*, because its national ruler will be everywhere the same—*Labour!* The pioneer of that new society is the International Working Men's Association.

July 23, 1870.

II

SECOND ADDRESS OF THE GENERAL COUNCIL ON THE FRANCO-PRUSSIAN WAR

In our first manifesto of the 23rd of July we said:

"The death-knell of the Second Empire has already sounded at Paris. It will end, as it began, by a parody. But let us not forget that it is the governments and the ruling classes of Europe who enabled Louis Napoleon to play during eighteen years the ferocious farce of the *Restored Empire.*"

Thus, even before war operations had actually set in, we treated the Bonapartist bubble as a thing of the past.

If we were not mistaken as to the vitality of the Second Empire, we were not wrong in our apprehension lest the German war should "lose its strictly defensive character and degenerate into a war against the French people." The war of defence ended, in point of fact, with the surrender of Louis Bonaparte, the Sedan capitulation, and the proclamation of the republic at Paris.[22] But long before these events, the very moment that the utter rottenness of the imperialist arms became evident, the Prussian military *camarilla* had resolved upon conquest. There lay an ugly obstacle in their way—*King William's own proclamations at the commencement of the war.* In his speech from the throne to the North German Diet, he had solemnly declared to make war upon the emperor of the French and not upon the French people. On August 11 he had issued a manifesto to the French nation, where he said: "The Emperor Napoleon having made by land and sea an attack on the German nation, which desired and still desires to live in peace with the French people, I have assumed the command of the German armies *to repel his aggression,* and I have been led by *military events to cross the frontiers of France.*" Not content to assert the defensive character of the war by the statement that he only assumed the command of the German armies *"to repel aggression,"* he added that he was only "led by military events" to cross the frontiers of

France. A defensive war does, of course, not exclude offensive operations, dictated by military events.

Thus, the pious king stood pledged before France and the world to a strictly defensive war. How to release him from his solemn pledge? The stage managers had to exhibit him as reluctantly yielding to the irresistible behest of the German nation. They at once gave the cue to the liberal German middle class, with its professors, its capitalists, its aldermen and its penmen. That middle class, which, in its struggles for civil liberty, had, from 1846 to 1870, been exhibiting an unexampled spectacle of irresolution, incapacity and cowardice, felt, of course, highly delighted to bestride the European scene as the roaring lion of German patriotism. It re-vindicated its civic independence by affecting to force upon the Prussian government the secret designs of that same government. It does penance for its long-continued and almost religious faith in Louis Bonaparte's infallibility, by shouting for the dismemberment of the French republic. Let us for a moment listen to the special pleadings of those stout-hearted patriots!

They dare not pretend that the people of Alsace and Lorraine pant for the German embrace; quite the contrary. To punish their French patriotism, Strasbourg, a town with an independent citadel commanding it, has for six days been wantonly and fiendishly bombarded by "German" explosive shells, setting it on fire, and killing great numbers of its defenceless inhabitants! Yet, the soil of those provinces once upon a time belonged to the whilom German empire. Hence, it seems, the soil and the human beings grown on it must be confiscated as imprescriptible German property. If the map of Europe is to be re-made in the antiquary's vein, let us by no means forget that the Elector of Brandenburg, for his Prussian dominions, was the vassal of the Polish republic.

The more knowing patriots, however, require Alsace and the German-speaking part of Lorraine as a "material guarantee" against French aggression. As this contemptible plea has bewildered many weak-minded people, we are bound to enter more fully upon it.

There is no doubt that the general configuration of Alsace, as compared with the opposite bank of the Rhine, and the presence

of a large fortified town like Strasbourg, about halfway between
Basle and Germersheim, very much favour a French invasion of
South Germany, while they offer peculiar difficulties to an invasion
of France from South Germany. There is, further, no doubt that
the addition of Alsace and German-speaking Lorraine would give
South Germany a much stronger frontier, inasmuch as she would
then be master of the crest of the Vosges mountains in its whole
length, and of the fortresses which cover its northern passes. If
Metz were annexed as well, France would certainly for the moment
be deprived of her two principal bases of operation against Germany, but that would not prevent her from constructing a fresh
one at Nancy or Verdun. While Germany owns Coblenz, Mayence,
Germersheim, Rastatt, and Ulm, all bases of operation against
France, and plentifully made use of in this war, with what show
of fair play can she begrudge France Strasbourg and Metz, the
only two fortresses of any importance she has on that side? Moreover, Strasbourg endangers South Germany only, while South
Germany is a separate power from North Germany. From 1792 to
1795 South Germany was never invaded from that direction, because
Prussia was a party to the war against the French Revolution; but
as soon as Prussia made a peace of her own in 1795, and left the
South to shift for itself, the invasions of South Germany with
Strasbourg for a base began and continued till 1809. The fact is, a
united Germany can always render Strasbourg and any French
army in Alsace innocuous by concentrating all her troops, as was
done in the present war, between Saarlouis and Landau, and advancing, or accepting battle, on the line of road between Mayence
and Metz. While the mass of the German troops is stationed there,
any French army advancing from Strasbourg into South Germany
would be outflanked, and have its communications threatened. If
the present campaign has proved anything, it is the facility of
invading France from Germany.

But, in good faith, is it not altogether an absurdity and an
anachronism to make military considerations the principle by which
the boundaries of nations are to be fixed? If this rule were to
prevail, Austria would still be entitled to Venetia and the line

of the Mincio, and France to the line of the Rhine, in order to protect Paris, which lies certainly more open to an attack from the northeast than Berlin does from the southwest. If limits are to be fixed by military interests, there will be no end to claims, because every military line is necessarily faulty, and may be improved by annexing some more outlying territory; and, moreover, they can never be fixed finally and fairly, because they always must be imposed by the conqueror upon the conquered, and consequently carry within them the seed of fresh wars.

Such is the lesson of all history. Thus with nations as with individuals. To deprive them of the power of offence, you must deprive them of the means of defence. You must not only garrote, but murder. If every conqueror took "material guarantees" for breaking the sinews of a nation, the first Napoleon did so by the Tilsit Treaty,[28] and the way he executed it against Prussia and the rest of Germany. Yet, a few years later, his gigantic power split like a rotten reed upon the German people. What are the "material guarantees" Prussia, in her wildest dreams, can or dare impose upon France, compared to the "material guarantees" the first Napoleon had wrenched from herself? The result will not prove the less disastrous. History will measure its retribution, not by the extent of the square miles conquered from France, but by the intensity of the crime of reviving, in the second half of the nineteenth century, *the policy of conquest!*

But, say the mouthpieces of Teutonic patriotism, you must not confound Germans with Frenchmen. What *we* want is not glory, but safety. The Germans are an essentially peaceful people. In their sober guardianship, conquest itself changes from a condition of future war into a pledge of perpetual peace. Of course, it is not Germans that invaded France in 1792, for the sublime purpose of bayonetting the revolution of the eighteenth century. It is not Germans that befouled their hands by the subjugation of Italy, the oppression of Hungary, and the dismemberment of Poland. Their present military system, which divides the whole able-bodied male population into two parts—one standing army on service, and another standing army on furlough, both equally bound in passive obedience to rulers by divine right—such a military system is, of course, "a material guarantee," for keeping the peace and the ultimate goal of civilising tendencies! In Germany, as everywhere else, the sycophants of the powers that be poison the popular mind by the incense of mendacious self praise.

Indignant as they pretend to be at the sight of French fortresses in Metz and Strasbourg, those German patriots see no harm in the vast system of Moscovite fortifications at Warsaw, Modlin, and Ivangorod. While gloating at the terrors of imperialist invasion, they blink at the infamy of autocratic tutelage.

As in 1865 promises were exchanged between Louis Bonaparte and Bismarck, so in 1870 promises have been exchanged between Gorchakov [24] and Bismarck. As Louis Bonaparte flattered himself that the War of 1866, resulting in the common exhaustion of Austria and Prussia, would make him the supreme arbiter of Germany, so Alexander flattered himself that the War of 1870, resulting in the common exhaustion of Germany and France, would make him the supreme arbiter of the Western continent. As the Second Empire thought the North German Confederation incompatible with its existence, so autocratic Russia must think herself endangered by a German empire under Prussian leadership. Such is the law of the old political system. Within its pale the gain of one state is the loss of the other. The tsar's paramount influence over Europe roots in his traditional hold on Germany. At a moment when in Russia herself volcanic social agencies threaten to shake the very base of autocracy, could the tsar afford to bear with such a loss of foreign prestige? Already the Moscovite journals repeat the language of the Bonapartist journals after the War of 1866.[25] Do the Teuton patriots really believe that liberty and peace will be guaranteed to Germany by forcing France into the arms of Russia? If the fortune of her arms, the arrogance of success, and dynastic intrigue lead Germany to a spoliation of French territory, there will then only remain two courses open to her. She must at all risks become the *avowed* tool of Russian aggrandisement, or, after some short respite, make again ready for another "defensive" war, not one of those new-fangled "localised" wars, but a *war of races*—a war with the combined Slavonian and Roman races.

The German working class have resolutely supported the war, which it was not in their power to prevent, as a war for German independence and the liberation of France and Europe from that pestilential incubus, the Second Empire. It was the German workmen who, together with the rural labourers, furnished the sinews and muscles of heroic hosts, leaving behind their half-starved families. Decimated by the battles abroad, they will be once more decimated by misery at home. In their turn they are now coming forward to ask for "guarantees"—guarantees that their immense sacrifices have not been bought in vain, that they have conquered liberty, that the victory over the imperialist armies will not, as in 1815, be turned into the defeat of the German people; and, as the first of these guarantees, they claim an *honourable peace for France,* and the *recognition of the French republic.*

The Central Committee of the German Socialist-Democratic Workmen's Party issued on September 5 a manifesto,[26] energetically insisting upon these guarantees.

"We," they say, "protest against the annexation of Alsace and Lorraine. And we are conscious of speaking in the name of the German working class. In the common interest of France and Germany, in the interest of western civilisation against eastern barbarism the German workmen will not patiently tolerate the annexation of Alsace and Lorraine.... We shall faithfully stand by our fellow workmen in all countries for the common international cause of the proletariat!"

Unfortunately, we cannot feel sanguine of their immediate success. If the French workmen amidst peace failed to stop the aggressor, are the German workmen more likely to stop the victor amidst the clamour of arms? The German workmen's manifesto demands the extradition of Louis Bonaparte as a common felon to the French republic. Their rulers are, on the contrary, already trying hard to restore him to the Tuileries as the best man to ruin France. However that may be, history will prove that the German working class are not made of the same malleable stuff as the German middle class. They will do their duty.

Like them, we hail the advent of the republic in France, but at the same time we labour under misgivings which we hope will prove groundless. That republic has not subverted the throne, but only taken its place become vacant. It has been proclaimed, not as a social conquest, but as a national measure of defence. It is in the hands of a Provisional Government composed partly of notorious Orleanists, partly of middle class republicans, upon some of whom the insurrection of June 1848 has left its indelible stigma. The division of labour amongst the members of that government looks awkward. The Orleanists have seized the strongholds of the army and the police, while to the professed republicans have fallen the talking departments. Some of their first acts go far to show that they have inherited from the empire, not only ruins, but also its dread of the working class. If eventual impossibilities are in wild phraseology promised in the name of the republic, is it not with a view to prepare the cry for a "possible" government! Is the republic, by some of its middle class undertakers, not intended to serve as a mere stop-gap and bridge over an Orleanist restoration?

The French working class moves, therefore, under circumstances of extreme difficulty. Any attempt at upsetting the new government in the present crisis, when the enemy is almost knocking at the doors of Paris, would be a desperate folly.[27] The French workmen must perform their duties as citizens; but, at the same time, they must not allow themselves to be swayed by the national *souvenirs* of 1792,[28] as the French peasants allowed themselves to be deluded by the national *souvenirs* of the First Empire.[29] They have not to recapitulate the past, but to build up the future. Let them calmly and resolutely improve the opportunities of republican liberty, for the work of their own class organisation. It will gift them with fresh herculean powers for the regeneration of France, and our common task—the emancipation of labour. Upon their energies and wisdom hinges the fate of the republic.

The English workmen have already taken measures to overcome, by a wholesome pressure from without, the reluctance of their government to recognise the French republic.[30] The present dilatoriness of the British government is probably intended to atone for the Anti-Jacobin war [1792] [31] and the former indecent haste in sanctioning the *coup d'état*. The English workmen call also upon their government to oppose by all its power the dismemberment of France, which a part of the English press is shameless enough to howl for. It is the same press that for twenty years deified Louis Bonaparte as the providence of Europe, that frantically cheered on the slaveholders to rebellion. [32] Now, as then, it drudges for the slaveholder.

Let the sections of the *International Working Men's Association* in every country stir the working classes to action. If they forsake their duty, if they remain passive, the present tremendous war will be but the harbinger of still deadlier international feuds, and lead in every nation to a renewed triumph over the workman by the lords of the sword, of the soil and of capital.

Vive la République!

The General Council

ROBERT APPLEGARTH, MARTIN J. BOON, FRED. BRADNICK, CAIHIL, JOHN HALES, WILLIAM HALES, GEORGE HARRIS, FRED. LESSNER, LAYSATINE, B. LUCRAFT, GEORGE MILNER, THOMAS MOTTERSHEAD, CHARLES MURRAY, GEORGE ODGER, JAMES PARNELL, PFANDER, RUHL, JOSEPH SHEPHERD, COWELL STEPNEY, STOLL, SCHMITZ.

Corresponding Secretaries:

EUGENE DUPONT, *for France*
HERMANN JUNG, *for Switzerland Holland and Spain*
A. SERRAILLER, *for Belgium*
KARL MARX, *for Germany and Russia*

GIOVANNI BORA, *for Italy*
ZEVY MAURICE, *for Hungary*
ANTON ZABICKI, *for Poland*
JAMES COHEN, *for Denmark*
J. G. ECCARIUS, *for the United States*

WILLIAM TOWNSEND, *Chairman*
JOHN WESTON, *Treasurer*
J. GEORGE ECCARIUS, *General Secretary*

Office: 256 HIGH HOLBORN, LONDON, W.C., *September 9, 1870*

III

ADDRESS OF THE GENERAL COUNCIL OF THE INTERNATIONAL WORKING MEN'S ASSOCIATION ON *THE CIVIL WAR IN FRANCE, 1871*

To All the Members of the Association in Europe and the United States

I

ON THE 4th of September, 1870, when the working men of Paris proclaimed the republic, which was almost instantaneously acclaimed throughout France, without a single voice of dissent, a cabal of place-hunting barristers, with Thiers for their statesman and Trochu for their general, took hold of the Hôtel de Ville. At that time they were imbued with so fanatical a faith in the mission of Paris to represent France in all epochs of historical crisis, that, to legitimate their usurped titles as governors of France, they thought it quite sufficient to produce their lapsed mandates as representatives of Paris. In our second address on the late war, five days after the rise of these men, we told you who they were. Yet, in the turmoil of surprise, with the real leaders of the working class still shut up in Bonapartist prisons and the Prussians already marching upon Paris, Paris bore with their assumption of power, on the express condition that it was to be wielded for the single purpose of national defence. Paris, however, was not to be defended without arming its working class, organising them into an effective force, and training their ranks by the war itself. But Paris armed was the revolution armed. A victory of Paris over the Prussian aggressor would have been a victory of the French workmen over the French capitalist and his state parasites. In this conflict between national duty and class interest, the Government of National

Defence did not hesitate one moment to turn into a Government of National Defection.

The first step they took was to send Thiers on a roving tour to all the courts of Europe, there to beg mediation by offering the barter of the republic for a king. Four months after the commencement of the siege, when they thought the opportune moment come for breaking the first word of capitulation, Trochu, in the presence of Jules Favre and others of his colleagues, addressed the assembled mayors of Paris in these terms:

"The first question put to me by my colleagues on the very evening of the 4th of September was this: Paris, can it, with any chance of success, stand a siege by the Prussian army? I did not hesitate to answer in the negative. Some of my colleagues here present will warrant the truth of my words and the persistence of my opinion. I told them, in these very terms, that, under the existing state of things, the attempt of Paris to hold out a siege by the Prussian army would be a folly. Without doubt, I added, it would be an heroic folly; but that would be all. . . . The events [managed by himself] have not given the lie to my prevision."

This nice little speech of Trochu was afterwards published by M. Carbon, one of the mayors present.

Thus, on the very evening of the proclamation of the republic, Trochu's "plan" was known to his colleagues to be the capitulation of Paris. If national defence had been more than a pretext for the personal government of Thiers, Favre and Co., the upstarts of the 4th of September would have abdicated on the 5th—would have initiated the Paris people into Trochu's "plan," and called upon them to surrender at once, or to take their own fate into their own hands. Instead of this, the infamous impostors resolved upon curing the heroic folly of Paris by a regimen of famine and broken heads, and to dupe her in the meanwhile by ranting manifestoes, holding forth that Trochu, "the governor of Paris, will never capitulate," and Jules Favre, the foreign minister, will "not cede an inch of our territory, nor a stone of our fortresses."

In a letter to Gambetta, that very same Jules Favre avows that what they were "defending" against were not the Prussian soldiers, but the working men of Paris. During the whole continuance of the siege the Bonapartist cut-throats, whom Trochu had wisely intrusted with the command of the Paris army, exchanged, in their intimate correspondence, ribald jokes at the well-understood mockery of defence. (See, for instance, the correspondence of Alphonse Simon Guiod, supreme commander of the artillery of the Army of Defence of Paris and Grand Cross of the Legion of Honour, to Suzanne, general of division of artillery, a correspondence published by the *Journal officiel* of the Commune.) The mask of imposture was at last dropped on the 28th of January, 1871. With the true heroism of utter self-debasement, the Government of National Defence, in their capitulation, came out as the government of France by Bismarck's prisoners—a part so base that Louis Bonaparte himself had, at Sedan, shrunk from accepting it. After the events of the 18th of March on their wild flight to Versailles, the *capitulards* left in the hands of Paris the documentary evidence of their treason, to destroy which, as the Commune says in its manifesto to the provinces, "those men would not recoil from battering Paris into a heap of ruins washed by a sea of blood."

To be eagerly bent upon such a consummation, some of the leading members of the Government of Defence had, besides, most peculiar reasons of their own.

Shortly after the conclusion of the armistice, M. Millière, one of the representatives of Paris to the National Assembly, now shot by express order of Jules Favre, published a series of authentic legal documents in proof that Jules Favre, living in concubinage with the wife of a drunken resident at Algiers, had, by a most daring concoction of forgeries, spread over many years, contrived to grasp, in the name of the children of his adultery, a large succession, which made him a rich man, and that, in a lawsuit undertaken by the legitimate heirs, he only escaped exposure by the connivance of the Bonapartist tribunals. As these dry legal documents were not to be got rid of by any amount of rhetorical horse-power, Jules Favre, for the first time in his life, held his tongue, quietly awaiting the outbreak of the civil war, in order, then, frantically to denounce the people of Paris as a band of escaped convicts in utter revolt against family, religion, order and property. This same forger had hardly got into power, after the 4th of September, when he sympathetically let loose upon society Pic and Taillefer, convicted, even under the empire, of forgery in the scandalous affair of the "Étendard." One of these men, Taillefer, having dared to return to Paris under the Commune, was at once reinstated in prison; and then Jules Favre exclaimed, from the tribune of the National Assembly, that Paris was setting free all her jailbirds!

Ernest Picard, the Joe Miller of the Government of National Defence, who appointed himself finance minister of the republic after having in vain striven to become the home minister of the empire, is the brother of one Arthur Picard, an individual expelled from the Paris *Bourse* as a blackleg (see report of the Prefecture of Police, dated 13th July, 1867), and convicted, on his own confession, of a theft of 300,000 francs, while manager of one of the branches of the *Société Générale*, Rue Palestro, No. 5 (see report of the Prefecture of Police, 11th December, 1868). This Arthur Picard was made by Ernest Picard the editor of his paper, *l'Electeur Libre*. While the common run of stockjobbers were led astray by the official lies of this finance office paper, Arthur was running backwards and forwards between the finance office and the *Bourse,* there to discount the disasters of the French army. The whole financial correspondence of that worthy pair of brothers fell into the hands of the Commune.

Jules Ferry, a penniless barrister before the 4th of September, contrived, as mayor of Paris during the siege, to job a fortune out of famine. The day on which he would have to give an account of his maladministration would be the day of his conviction.

These men, then, could find in the ruins of Paris only their tickets-of-leave: they were the very men Bismarck wanted. With the help of some shuffling of cards, Thiers, hitherto the secret prompter of the government, now appeared at its head, with the ticket-of-leave men for his ministers.

Thiers, that monstrous gnome, has charmed the French bourgeoisie for almost half a century, because he is the most consummate intellectual expression of their own class corruption. Before he became a statesman he had already proved his lying powers as an historian. The chronicle of his public life is the record of the misfortunes of France. Banded, before 1830, with the republicans, he slipped into office under Louis Philippe by betraying his protector Lafitte, ingratiating himself with the king by exciting mob riots against the clergy, during which the church of Saint Germain l'Auxerrois and the Archbishop's palace were plundered, and by acting the minister-spy upon, and the jail-*accoucheur* of the Duchess de Berri. The massacre of the republicans in the Rue Transnonain,[33] and the subsequent infamous laws of September against the press and the right of association, were his work. Reappearing as the chief of the cabinet in March 1840, he astonished France with his plan of fortifying France. To the republicans, who denounced this plan as a sinister plot against the liberty of Paris, he replied from the tribune of the Chamber of Deputies:

"What! to fancy that any works of fortification could ever endanger liberty! And first of all you calumniate any possible government in supposing that it could some day attempt to maintain itself by bombarding the capital; . . . but that government would be a hundred times more impossible after its victory than before."

Indeed, no government would ever have dared to bombard Paris from the forts but that government which had previously surrendered these forts to the Prussians.

When King Bomba[34] tried his hand at Palermo, in January 1848, Thiers, then long since out of office, again rose in the Chamber of Deputies:

"You know, gentlemen, what is happening at Palermo. You, all of you, shake with horror [in the parliamentary sense] on hearing that during forty-eight hours a large town has been bombarded—by whom? Was it by a foreign enemy exercising the rights of war? No, gentlemen, it was by its own government. And why? Because the unfortunate town demanded its right. Well, then, for the demand of its rights it has got forty-eight hours of bombardment. . . . Allow me to appeal to the opinion of Europe. It is doing a service to mankind to arise, and to make reverberate, from what is perhaps the greatest tribune in Europe, some words [indeed words] of indignation against such acts. . . . When the Regent Espartero, who had rendered services to his country [which M. Thiers never did] intended bombarding Barcelona, in order to suppress its insurrection, there arose from all parts of the world a general outcry of indignation."

Eighteen months afterwards, M. Thiers was amongst the fiercest defenders of the bombardment of Rome by a French army. In fact, the fault of King Bomba seems to have consisted in this only, that he limited his bombardment to forty-eight hours.

A few days before the Revolution of February, fretting at the long exile from place and pelf to which Guizot had condemned him, and sniffing in the air the scent of an approaching popular commotion, Thiers, in that pseudo-heroic style which won him the nickname of *Mirabeau-mouche,* declared, to the Chamber of Deputies:

"I am of the party of revolution, not only in France, but in Europe. I wish the government of the revolution to remain in the hands of moderate men . . . but if that government should fall into the hands of ardent minds, even into those of radicals, I shall, for all that, not desert my cause. I shall always be of the party of the revolution."

The Revolution of February came. Instead of displacing the Guizot Cabinet by the Thiers Cabinet, as the little man had dreamt, it superseded Louis Philippe by the republic. On the first day of the popular victory he carefully hid himself, forgetting that the contempt of the working men screened him from their hatred. Still, with his legendary courage, he continued to shy the public stage, until the June massacres [36] had cleared it for his sort of action. Then he became the leading mind of the "Party of Order" and its parliamentary republic, that anonymous interregnum, in which all the rival factions of the ruling class conspired together to crush the people, and conspired against each other to restore to each of them its own monarchy. Then, as now, Thiers denounced the republicans as the only obstacle to the consolidation of the republic; then, as now, he spoke to the republic as the hangman spoke to Don Carlos: [86] "I shall assassinate thee, but for thy own good." Now, as then, he will have to exclaim on the day after his victory: *L'Empire est fait*—the empire is consummated. Despite his hypocritical homilies about necessary liberties and his personal grudge against Louis Bonaparte, who had made a dupe of him, and kicked out parliamentarism—and outside of its factitious atmosphere the little man is conscious of withering into nothingness—he had a hand in all the infamies of the Second Empire, from the occupation of Rome by French troops to the war with Prussia, which he incited by his fierce invective against German unity—not as a cloak of Prussian despotism, but as an encroachment upon the vested right of France in German disunion. Fond of brandishing with his dwarfish arms in the face of Europe the sword of the first Napoleon, whose historical shoeblack he had become,[87] his foreign policy always culminated in the utter humiliation of France, from the London convention of 1840 to the Paris capitulation of 1871, and the present civil war, where he hounds on the prisoners of Sedan and Metz against Paris by special permission of Bismarck. Despite his versatility of talent and shiftiness of purpose, this man has his whole lifetime been wedded to the most fossil routine. It is self-evident that to him the deeper undercurrents of modern society remained forever hidden; but even the most palpable changes on its surface were abhorrent to a brain all the vitality of which had fled to the tongue. Thus he never tired of denouncing as a sacrilege any deviation from the old French protective system.[88] When a minister of Louis Philippe, he railed at railways as a wild chimera; and when in opposition under Louis Bonaparte, he branded as a profanation every attempt to reform the rotten French army system. Never in his long political career has he been guilty of a single— even the smallest—measure of any practical use. Thiers was consistent only in his greed for wealth and his hatred of the men that produce it. Having entered his first ministry under Louis Philippe poor as Job, he left it a millionaire. His last ministry under the same king (of the 1st of March, 1840) exposed him to public taunts of peculation in the Chamber of Deputies, to which he was content to reply by tears—a commodity he deals in as freely as Jules Favre, or any other crocodile. At Bordeaux his first measure for saving France from impending financial ruin was to endow himself with three millions a year, the first and the last word of the "Economical Republic," the vista of which he had opened to his Paris electors in 1869. One of his former colleagues of the Chamber of Deputies of 1830, himself a capitalist and, nevertheless, a devoted member of the Paris Commune, M. Beslay, lately addressed Thiers thus in a public placard: "The enslavement of labour by capital has always been the cornerstone of your policy, and from the very day you saw the Republic of Labour installed at the Hôtel de Ville, you have never ceased to cry out to France: 'These are criminals!'" A master in small state roguery, a virtuoso in perjury and treason, a craftsman in all the petty stratagems, cunning devices, and base perfidies of parliamentary party warfare; never scrupling, when out of office, to fan a revolution, and to stifle it in blood when at the helm of the state; with class prejudices standing him in the place of ideas, and vanity in the place of a heart; his private life as infamous as his public life is odious—even now, when playing the part of a French Sulla, he cannot help setting off the abomination of his deeds by the ridicule of his ostentation.

The capitulation of Paris, by surrendering to Prussia not only Paris, but all France, closed the long-continued intrigues of treason with the enemy, which the usurpers of the 4th September had begun, as Trochu himself said, on that very same day. On the other hand, it initiated the civil war they were now to wage, with the assistance of Prussia, against the republic and Paris. The trap was laid in the very terms of the capitulation. At that time above one-third of the territory was in the hands of the enemy, the capital was cut off from the provinces, all communications were disorganised. To elect under such circumstances a real representation of France was impossible, unless ample time were given for preparation. In view of this, the capitulation stipulated that a National Assembly must be elected within eight days; so that in many parts of France the news of the impending election arrived on its eve only. This assembly, moreover, was, by an express clause of the capitulation, to be elected for the sole purpose of deciding on peace or war, and, eventually, to conclude a treaty of peace. The population could not but feel that the terms of the armistice rendered the continuation of the war impossible, and that for sanctioning the peace imposed by Bismarck, the worst men in France were the best. But not content with these precautions, Thiers even before the secret of the armistice had been broached to Paris, set out for an electioneering tour through the provinces, there to galvanise back into life the Legitimist party, which now, along with the Orleanists, had to take the place of the then impossible Bonapartists. He was not afraid of them. Impossible as a government of modern France, and, therefore, contemptible as rivals, what party were more eligible as tools of counter-revolution than the party whose action, in the words of Thiers himself (Chamber of Deputies, 5th January, 1833), "had always been confined to the three resources of foreign invasion, civil war, and anarchy"? They verily believed in the advent of their long-expected retrospective millennium. There were the heels of foreign invasion trampling upon France; there was the downfall of an empire, and the captivity of a Bonaparte; and there they were themselves. The wheel of history had evidently rolled back to stop at the "Chambre introuvable" [39] of 1816. In the assemblies of the republic, 1848 to 1851, they had been represented by their educated and trained parliamentary champions; it was the rank-and-file of the party which now rushed in—all the Pourceaugnacs of France.

As soon as this Assembly of "Rurals" [40] had met at Bordeaux, Thiers made it clear to them that the peace preliminaries must be assented to at once, without even the honours of a parliamentary debate, as the only condition on which Prussia would permit them to open the war against the republic and Paris, its stronghold. The counter-revolution had, in fact, no time to lose. The Second Empire had more than doubled the national debt, and plunged all the large towns into heavy municipal debts. The war had fearfully swelled the liabilities, and mercilessly ravaged the resources of the nation. To complete the ruin, the Prussian Shylock was there with his bond for the keep of half a million of his soldiers on French soil, his indemnity of five milliards, and interest at 5 per cent on the unpaid instalments thereof. Who was to pay the bill? It was only by the violent overthrow of the republic that the appropriators of wealth could hope to shift on to the shoulders of its producers the cost of a war which they, the appropriators, had themselves originated. Thus, the immense ruin of France spurred on these patriotic representatives of land and capital, under the very eyes and patronage of the invader, to graft upon the foreign war a civil war—a slaveholders' rebellion.

There stood in the way of this conspiracy one great obstacle—Paris. To disarm Paris was the first condition of success. Paris was therefore summoned by Thiers to surrender its arms. Then Paris was exasperated by the frantic anti-republican demonstrations of the "Rural" Assembly and by Thiers' own equivocations about the legal status of the republic; by the threat to decapitate and decapitalise Paris; the appointment of Orleanist ambassadors; Dufaure's laws on over-due commercial bills and house rents, inflicting ruin on the commerce and industry of Paris; Pouyer-Quertier's tax of two centimes upon every copy of every imaginable publication; the sentences of death against Blanqui and Flourens; the suppression of the republican journals; the transfer of the National Assembly to Versailles; the renewal of the state of siege declared by Palikao, and expired on the 4th of September; the appointment of Vinoy, the *Décembriseur,* as governor of Paris—of Valentin, the imperialist *gendarme,* as its prefect of police—and of D'Aurelles de Paladine, the Jesuit general, as the commander-in-chief of its National Guard.

And now we have to address a question to M. Thiers and the men of national defence, his under-strappers. It is known that, through the agency of M. Pouyer-Quertier, his finance ministers, Thiers had contracted a loan of two milliards. Now, is it true or not—

1. That the business was so managed that a consideration of several hundred millions was secured for the private benefit of Thiers, Jules Favre, Ernest Picard, Pouyer-Quertier, and Jules Simon? and—

2. That no money was to be paid down until after the "pacification" of Paris?

At all events, there must have been something very pressing in the matter, for Thiers and Jules Favre, in the name of the majority of the Bordeaux Assembly, unblushingly solicited the immediate occupation of Paris by Prussian troops. Such, however, was not the game of Bismarck, as he sneeringly, and in public, told the admiring Frankfort philistines on his return to Germany.

II

Armed Paris was the only serious obstacle in the way of the counter-revolutionary conspiracy. Paris was, therefore, to be disarmed. On this point the Bordeaux Assembly was sincerity itself. If the roaring rant of its Rurals had not been audible enough, the surrender of Paris by Thiers to the tender mercies of the triumvirate of Vinoy the *Décembriseur*, Valentin the Bonapartist *gendarme*, and Aurelles de Paladine the Jesuit general, would have cut off even the last subterfuge of doubt. But while insultingly exhibiting the true purpose of the disarmament of Paris, the conspirators asked her to lay down her arms on a pretext which was the most glaring, the most barefaced of lies. The artillery of the Paris National Guard, said Thiers, belonged to the state, and to the state it must be returned. The fact was this: From the very day of the capitulation, by which Bismarck's prisoners had signed the surrender of France, but reserved to themselves a numerous bodyguard for the express purpose of cowing Paris, Paris stood on the watch. The National Guard reorganised themselves and intrusted their supreme control to a Central Committee elected by their whole body, save some fragments of the old Bonapartist formations. On the eve of the entrance of the Prussians into Paris, the Central Committee took measures for the removal to Montmartre, Belleville, and La Villette of the cannon and *mitrailleuses* treacherously abandoned by the *capitulards* in and about the very quarters the Prussians were to occupy. That artillery had been furnished by the subscriptions of the National Guard. As their private property, it was officially recognised in the capitulation of the 28th of January, and on that very title exempted from the general surrender, into the hands of the conqueror, of arms belonging to the government. And Thiers was so utterly destitute of even the flimsiest pretext for initiating the war against Paris, that he had to resort to the flagrant lie of the artillery of the National Guard being state property!

The seizure of her artillery was evidently but to serve as the preliminary to the general disarmament of Paris, and, therefore, of the Revolution of the 4th of September. But that revolution had become the legal status of France. The republic, its work, was recognised by the conqueror in the terms of the capitulation. After the capitulation, it was acknowledged by all the foreign powers, and in its name the National Assembly had been summoned. The Paris working men's revolution of the 4th of September was the only legal title of the National Assembly seated at Bordeaux, and of its executive. Without it, the National Assembly would at once have to give way to the *Corps Législatif* elected in 1869 by universal suffrage under French, not under Prussian, rule, and forcibly dispersed by the arm of the revolution. Thiers and his ticket-of-leave men would have had to capitulate for safe conducts signed by Louis Bonaparte, to save them from a voyage to Cayenne.[41] The National Assembly, with its power of attorney to settle the terms of peace with Prussia, was but an incident of that revolution, the true embodiment of which was still armed Paris, which had initiated it, undergone for it a five-months' siege, with its horrors of famine, and made her prolonged resistance, despite Trochu's plan, the basis of an obstinate war of defence in the provinces. And Paris was now either to lay down her arms at the insulting behest of the rebellious slaveholders of Bordeaux, and acknowledge that her Revolution of the 4th of September meant nothing but a simple transfer of power from Louis Bonapart to his royal rivals; or she had to stand forward as the self-sacrificing champion of France, whose salvation from ruin and whose regeneration were impossible without the revolutionary overthrow of the political and social conditions that had engendered the Second Empire, and, under its fostering care, matured into utter rottenness. Paris, emaciated by a five-months' famine, did not hesitate one moment. She heroically resolved to run all the hazards of a resistance against the French conspirators, even with Prussian cannon frowning upon her from her own forts. Still, in its abhor-rence of the civil war into which Paris was to be goaded, the Cen-tral Committee continued to persist in a merely defensive attitude, despite the provocations of the Assembly, the usurpations of the Executive, and the menacing concentration of troops in and around Paris.

Thiers opened the civil war by sending Vinoy, at the head of a multitude of *sergents-de-ville* and some regiments of the line, upon a nocturnal expedition against Montmartre, there to seize, by sur-prise, the artillery of the National Guard. It is well known how this attempt broke down before the resistance of the National Guard and the fraternisation of the line with the people. Aurelles de Paladine had printed beforehand his bulletin of victory, and Thiers held ready the placards announcing his measures of *coup d'état.* Now these had to be replaced by Thiers' appeals, imparting his magnanimous resolve to leave the National Guard in the possession of their arms, with which, he said, he felt sure they would rally round the government against the rebels. Out of 300,000 National Guards only 300 responded to this summons to rally round little Thiers against themselves. The glorious working men's Revolution of the 18th March took undisputed sway of Paris. The Central Com-mittee was its provisional government. Europe seemed, for a mo-ment, to doubt whether its recent sensational performances of state and war had any reality in them or whether they were the dreams of a long bygone past.

From the 18th of March to the entrance of the Versailles troops into Paris, the proletarian revolution remained so free from the acts of violence in which the revolutions, and still more the counter-revolutions, of the "better classes" abound, that no facts were left to its opponents to cry out about, but the execution of Generals Lecomte and Clement Thomas, and the affair of the Place Ven-dôme.

One of the Bonapartist officers engaged in the nocturnal attempt against Montmartre, General Lecomte, had four times ordered the 81st line regiment to fire at an unarmed gathering in the Place Pigalle, and on their refusal fiercely insulted them. Instead of shooting women and children, his own men shot him. The inveterate habits acquired by the soldiery under the training of the enemies of the working class are, of course, not likely to change the very moment these soldiers change sides. The same men executed Clement Thomas.

"General" Clement Thomas, a malcontent ex-quartermaster-sergeant, had, in the latter times of Louis Philippe's reign, enlisted at the office of the republican newspaper *Le National*, there to serve in the double capacity of responsible man-of-straw (*gérant responsable*)[42] and of duelling bully to that very combative journal. After the Revolution of February, the men of the *National* having got into power, they metamorphosed this old quarter-master-sergeant into a general on the eve of the butchery of June, of which he, like Jules Favre, was one of the sinister plotters, and became one of the most dastardly executioners. Then he and his generalship disappeared for a long time, to again rise to the surface on the 1st November, 1870. The day before[43] the Government of Defence, caught at the Hôtel de Ville, had solemnly pledged their parole to Blanqui, Flourens, and other representatives of the working class, to abdicate their usurped power into the hands of a commune to be freely elected by Paris. Instead of keeping their word, they let loose on Paris the Bretons of Trochu, who now replaced the Corsicans of Bonaparte. General Tamisier alone, refusing to sully his name by such a breach of faith, resigned the commandership-in-chief of the National Guard, and in his place Clement Thomas for once became again a general. During the whole of his tenure of command, he made war, not upon the Prussians, but upon the Paris National Guard. He prevented their general armament, pitted the bourgeois battalions against the working men's battalions, weeded out the officers hostile to Trochu's "plan," and disbanded, under the stigma of cowardice, the very same proletarian battalions whose heroism has now astonished their most inveterate enemies. Clement Thomas felt quite proud of having reconquered his June pre-eminence as the personal enemy of the working class of Paris. Only a few days before the 18th of March, he laid before the War Minister, Leflô, a plan of his own for "finishing off *la fine fleur* [the

the headquarters of the National Guard in the Place Vendôme. In reply to their pistol-shots, the regular *sommations* (the French equivalent of the English Riot Act) were made, and, proving ineffective, fire was commanded by the general of the National Guard. One volley dispersed into wild flight the silly coxcombs, who expected that the mere exhibition of their "respectability" would have the same effect upon the Revolution of Paris as Joshua's trumpets upon the walls of Jericho. The runaways left behind them two National Guards killed, nine severely wounded (among them a member of the Central Committee), and the whole scene of their exploit strewn with revolvers, daggers, and sword-canes, in evidence of the "unarmed" character of their "pacific" demonstration. When, on the 13th of June, 1849, the National Guard made a really pacific demonstration in protest against the felonious assault of French troops upon Rome, Changarnier, then general of the Party of Order, was acclaimed by the National Assembly, and especially by M. Thiers, as the saviour of society, for having launched his troops from all sides upon these unarmed men, to shoot and sabre them down, and to trample them under their horses' feet. Paris, then, was placed under a state of siege. Dufaure hurried through the Assembly new laws of repression. New arrests, new proscriptions— a new reign of terror set in. But the lower orders manage these things otherwise. The Central Committee of 1871 simply ignored the heroes of the "pacific demonstration"; so much so, that only two days later they were enabled to muster under Admiral Saisset, for that *armed* demonstration, crowned by the famous stampede to Versailles. In their reluctance to continue the civil war opened by Thiers' burglarious attempt on Montmartre, the Central Committee made themselves, this time, guilty of a decisive mistake in not at once marching upon Versailles, then completely helpless, and thus putting an end to the conspiracies of Thiers and his Rurals. Instead of this, the Party of Order was again allowed to try its strength at the ballot box, on the 26th of March,[45] the day of the election of the Commune. Then, in the *mairies* of Paris, they exchanged bland words of conciliation with their too generous conquerors, muttering in their hearts solemn vows to exterminate them in due time.

Now, look at the reverse of the medal. Thiers opened his second campaign against Paris in the beginning of April. The first batch of Parisian prisoners brought into Versailles was subjected to revolting atrocities, while Ernest Picard, with his hands in his trousers' pockets, strolled about jeering them, and while Mesdames Thiers and Favre, in the midst of their ladies of honour (?) applauded, from the balcony, the outrages of the Versailles mob. The captured soldiers of the line were massacred in cold blood; our brave friend, General Duval, the iron-founder, was shot without any form of trial. Galifet, the kept man of his wife, so notorious for her shameless exhibitions at the orgies of the Second Empire, boasted in a proclamation of having commanded the murder of a small troop of National Guards, with their captain and lieutenant, surprised and disarmed by his Chasseurs. Vinoy, the runaway, was appointed by Thiers, Grand Cross of the Legion of Honour, for his general order to shoot down every soldier of the line taken in the ranks of the Federals. Desmarêt, the Gendarme, was decorated for the treacherous butcher-like chopping in pieces of the high-souled and chivalrous Flourens, who had saved the heads of the Government of Defence on the 31st of October, 1870. "The encouraging particulars" of his assassination were triumphantly expatiated upon by Thiers in the National Assembly. With the elated vanity of a parliamentary Tom Thumb, permitted to play the part of a Tamerlane, he denied the rebels against his littleness every right of civilised warfare, up to the right of neutrality for ambulances. Nothing more horrid than that monkey allowed for a time to give full fling to his tigerish instincts, as foreseen by Voltaire.

After the decree of the Commune of the 7th April ordering reprisals and declaring it to be its duty "to protect Paris against the cannibal exploits of the Versailles banditti, and to demand an eye for an eye, a tooth for a tooth," Thiers did not stop the barbarous treatment of prisoners, moreover insulting them in his bulletins as follows: "Never have more degraded countenances of a degraded democracy met the afflicted gazes of honest men,"—honest, like Thiers himself and his ministerial ticket-of-leave men. Still the shooting of prisoners was suspended for a time. Hardly, however, had Thiers and his Decembrist generals become aware that the Communal decree of reprisals was but an empty threat, that even their gendarme spies caught in Paris under the disguise of National Guards, that even *sergents-de-ville,* taken with incendiary shells upon them, were spared—when the wholesale shooting of prisoners was resumed and carried on uninterruptedly to the end. Houses to which National Guards had fled were surrounded by gendarmes, inundated with petroleum (which here occurs for the first time in this war), and then set fire to, the charred corpses being afterwards brought out by the ambulance of the Press at the Ternes. Four National Guards having surrendered to a troop of mounted Chasseurs at Belle Epine, on the 25th of April, were afterwards shot down, one after another, by the captain, a worthy man of Gallifet's. One of his four victims, left for dead, Scheffer, crawled back to the Parisian outposts, and deposed to this fact before a commission of the Commune. When Tolain interpellated the War Minister upon the report of this commission, the Rurals drowned his voice and forbade Leflô to answer. It would be an insult to their "glorious" army to speak of its deeds. The flippant tone in which Thiers' bulletins announced the bayoneting of the Federals surprised asleep at Moulin Saquet, and the wholesale fusillades at Clamart shocked the nerves even of the not over-sensitive London *Times.* But it would be ludicrous today to attempt recounting the merely preliminary atrocities committed by the bombarders of Paris and the fomenters of a slaveholders' rebellion protected by foreign invasion. Amidst all these horrors, Thiers, forgetful of his parliamentary laments on the terrible responsibility weighing down his dwarfish shoulders, boasts in his bulletins that *l'Assemblée siège paisiblement* (the Assembly continues meeting in peace), and proves by his constant carousals, now with Decembrist generals, now with German princes, that his digestion is not troubled in the least, not even by the ghosts of Lecomte and Clement Thomas.

III

On the dawn of the 18th of March, Paris arose to the thunderburst of "Vive la Commune!" What is the Commune, that sphinx so tantalising to the bourgeois mind?

"The proletarians of Paris," said the Central Committee in its manifesto of the 18th March, "amidst the failures and treasons of the ruling classes, have understood that the hour has struck for them to save the situation by taking into their own hands the direction of public affairs.... They have understood that it is their imperious duty and their absolute right to render themselves masters of their own destinies, by seizing upon the governmental power." But the working class cannot simply lay hold of the ready-made state machinery, and wield it for its own purposes.[46]

The centralised state power, with its ubiquitous organs of standing army, police, bureaucracy, clergy, and judicature—organs wrought after the plan of a systematic and hierarchic division of labour—originates from the days of absolute monarchy, serving nascent middle class society as a mighty weapon in its struggles against feudalism. Still, its development remained clogged by all manner of mediæval rubbish, seignorial rights, local privileges, municipal and guild monopolies and provincial constitutions. The gigantic broom of the French Revolution of the eighteenth century swept away all these relics of bygone times, thus clearing simultaneously the social soil of its last hindrances to the superstructure of the modern state edifice raised under the First Empire, itself the offspring of the coalition wars [47] of old semi-feudal Europe against modern France. During the subsequent *régimes* the government, placed under parliamentary control—that is, under the direct control of the propertied classes—became not only a hotbed of huge national debts and crushing taxes; with its irresistible allurements of place, pelf, and patronage, it became not only the bone of contention between the rival factions and adventurers of the ruling classes; but its political character changed simultaneously with the economic changes of society. At the same pace at which the progress of modern industry developed, widened, intensified the class antagonism between capital and labour, the state power assumed more and more the character of the national power of capital over labour, of a public force organised for social enslavement, of an engine of class despotism. After every revolution marking a progressive phase in the class struggle, the purely repressive character of the state power stands out in bolder and bolder relief. The Revolution of 1830, resulting in the transfer of government from the landlords to the capitalists, transferred it from the more remote to the more direct antagonists of the working men. The bourgeois republicans, who, in the name of the Revolution of February, took the state power, used it for the June massacres, in order to convince the working class that "social" republic meant the republic ensuring their social subjection, and in order to convince the royalist bulk of the bourgeois and landlord class that they might safely leave the cares and emoluments of government to the bourgeois "republicans." However, after their one heroic exploit of June, the bourgeois republicans had, from the front, to fall back to the rear of the "Party of Order"—a combination formed by all the rival fractions and factions of the appropriating class in their now openly declared antagonism to the producing classes. The proper form of their joint-stock government was the *parliamentary republic*, with Louis Bonaparte for its president. Theirs was a *régime* of avowed class terrorism and deliberate insult towards the "vile multitude." If the parliamentary republic, as M. Thiers said, "divided them [the different fractions of the ruling class] least," it opened an abyss between that class and the whole body of society outside their spare ranks. The restraints by which their own divisions had under former *régimes* still checked the state power, were removed by their union; and in view of the threatening upheaval of the proletariat, they now used that state power mercilessly and ostentatiously as the national war engine of capital against labour. In their uninterrupted crusade against the producing masses they were, however, bound not only to invest the executive with continually increased powers of repression, but at the same time to divest their own parliamentary stronghold—the National Assembly—one by one, of all its own means of defence against the Executive. The Executive, in the person of Louis Bonaparte, turned them out. The natural offspring of the "Party of Order" republic was the Second Empire.

The empire, with the *coup d'état* for its certificate of birth, universal suffrage for its sanction, and the sword for its sceptre, professed to rest upon the peasantry, the large mass of producers not directly involved in the struggle of capital and labour. It professed to save the working class by breaking down parliamentarism, and, with it, the undisguised subserviency of government to the propertied classes. It professed to save the propertied classes by upholding their economic supremacy over the working class; and, finally, it professed to unite all classes by reviving for all the chimera of national glory. In reality, it was the only form of government possible at a time when the bourgeoisie had already lost, and the working class had not yet acquired, the faculty of ruling the nation. It was acclaimed throughout the world as the saviour of society. Under its sway, bourgeois society, freed from political cares, attained a development unexpected even by itself. Its industry and commerce expanded to colossal dimensions; financial swindling celebrated cosmopolitan orgies; the misery of the masses was set off by a shameless display of gorgeous, meretricious and debased luxury. The state power, apparently soaring high above society, was at the same time itself the greatest scandal of that society and the very hotbed of all its corruptions. Its own rottenness, and the rottenness of the society it had saved, were laid bare by the bayonet of Prussia, herself eagerly bent upon transferring the supreme seat of that *régime* from Paris to Berlin. Imperialism [48] is, at the same time, the most prostitute and the ultimate form of the state power which nascent middle class society had commenced to elaborate as a means of its own emancipation from feudalism, and which full-grown bourgeois society had finally transformed into a means for the enslavement of labour by capital.

The direct antithesis to the empire was the Commune. The cry of "social republic" with which the Revolution of February was ushered in by the Paris proletariat, did but express a vague aspiration after a republic that was not only to supersede the monarchical form of class rule, but class rule itself. The Commune was the positive form of that republic.

Paris, the central seat of the old governmental power, and, at the same time, the social stronghold of the French working class, had risen in arms against the attempt of Thiers and the Rurals to restore and perpetuate that old governmental power bequeathed to them by the empire. Paris could resist only because, in consequence of the siege, it had got rid of the army, and replaced it by a National Guard, the bulk of which consisted of working men. This fact was now to be transformed into an institution. The first decree of the Commune, therefore, was the suppression of the standing army, and the substitution for it of the armed people.

The Commune was formed of the municipal councillors, chosen by universal suffrage in the various wards of the town, responsible and revocable at short terms. The majority of its members were naturally working men, or acknowledged representatives of the working class. The Commune was to be a working, not a parliamentary body, executive and legislative at the same time.[49] Instead of continuing to be the agent of the Central Government, the police was at once stripped of its political attributes, and turned into the responsible and at all times revocable agent of the Commune. So were the officials of all other branches of the administration. From the members of the Commune downwards, the public service had to be done at *workmen's wages*. The vested interests and the representation allowances of the high dignitaries of state disappeared along with the high dignitaries themselves. Public functions ceased to be the private property of the tools of the Central Government. Not only municipal administration, but the whole initiative hitherto exercised by the state was laid into the hands of the Commune.

Having once got rid of the standing army and the police, the physical force elements of the old government, the Commune was anxious to break the spiritual force of repression, the "parson-power," by the disestablishment and disendowment of all churches as proprietary bodies. The priests were sent back to the recesses of private life, there to feed upon the alms of the faithful in imitation of their predecessors, the apostles. The whole of the educational institutions were opened to the people gratuitously, and at the same time cleared of all interference of church and state. Thus, not only was education made accessible to all, but science itself freed from the fetters which class prejudice and governmental force had imposed upon it.

The judicial functionaries were to be divested of that sham independence which had but served to mask their abject subserviency to all succeeding governments to which, in turn, they had taken, and broken, the oaths of allegiance. Like the rest of public servants, magistrates and judges were to be elective, responsible and revocable.

The Paris Commune was, of course, to serve as a model to all the great industrial centres of France. The communal *régime* once established in Paris and the secondary centres, the old centralised government would in the provinces, too, have to give way to the self-government of the producers. In a rough sketch of national organisation which the Commune had no time to develop, it states clearly that the Commune was to be the political form of even the smallest country hamlet, and that in the rural districts the standing army was to be replaced by a national militia, with an extremely short term of service. The rural communes of every district were to administer their common affairs by an assembly of delegates in the central town, and these district assemblies were again to send deputies to the National Delegation in Paris, each delegate to be at any time revocable and bound by the *mandat impératif* (formal instructions) of his constituents. The few but important functions which still would remain for a central government were not to be suppressed, as has been intentionally misstated, but were to be discharged by Communal and therefore strictly responsible agents. The unity of the nation was not to be broken, but, on the contrary, to be organised by the Communal Constitution, and to become a reality by the destruction of the state power which claimed to be the embodiment of that unity independent of, and superior to, the nation itself, from which it was but a parasitic excrescence. While the merely repressive organs of the old governmental power were to be amputated, its legitimate functions were to be wrested from an authority usurping pre-eminence over society itself, and restored to the responsible agents of society. Instead of deciding once in three or six years which member of the ruling class was to mis-represent the people in Parliament,[50] universal suffrage was to serve the people, constituted in Communes, as individual suffrage serves every other employer in the search for the workmen and managers in his business. And it is well known that companies, like indi-viduals, in matters of real business generally know how to put the right man in the right place, and, if they for once make a mistake, to redress it promptly. On the other hand, nothing could be more foreign to the spirit of the Commune than to supersede universal suffrage by hierarchic investiture.

It is generally the fate of completely new historical creations to be mistaken for the counterpart of older and even defunct forms of social life, to which they may bear a certain likeness. Thus, this new Commune, which breaks the modern state power, has been mistaken for a reproduction of the mediæval Communes, which first preceded, and afterwards became the substratum of, that very state power.—The Communal Constitution has been mistaken for an attempt to break up into a federation of small states, as dreamt of by Montesquieu and the Girondins,[51] that unity of great nations which, if originally brought about by political force, has now be-come a powerful coefficient of social production.—The antagonism of the Commune against the state power has been mistaken for an exaggerated form of the ancient struggle against over-centralisation. Peculiar historical circumstances may have prevented the classical development, as in France, of the bourgeois form of government, and may have allowed, as in England, to complete the great central state organs by corrupt vestries, jobbing councillors, and ferocious poor-law guardians in the towns, and virtually hereditary magis-trates in the counties. The Communal Constitution would have restored to the social body all the forces hitherto absorbed by the state parasite feeding upon, and clogging the free movement of, society. By this one act it would have initiated the regeneration of France. The provincial French middle class saw in the Commune an attempt to restore the sway their order had held over the coun-try under Louis Philippe, and which, under Louis Napoleon, was supplanted by the pretended rule of the country over the towns. In reality, the Communal Constitution brought the rural producers under the intellectual lead of the central towns of their districts, and there secured to them, in the working men, the natural trustees of their interests. The very existence of the Commune involved, as a matter of course, local municipal liberty, but no longer as a check upon the now superseded state power. It could only enter into the head of a Bismarck, who, when not engaged on his intrigues of blood and iron, always likes to resume his old trade, so befitting his mental calibre, of contributor to *Kladderadatsch* (the Berlin *Punch*), it could only enter into such a head to ascribe to the Paris Commune aspirations after that caricature of the old French municipal organisation of 1791, the Prussian municipal constitution which degrades the town governments to mere secondary wheels in the police machinery of the Prussian state. The Commune made that catchword of bourgeois revolutions, cheap government, a reality by destroying the two greatest sources of expenditure—the standing army and state functionarism. Its very existence presupposed the non-existence of monarchy, which, in Europe at least, is the normal incumbrance and indispensable cloak of class rule. It supplied the republic with the basis of really democratic institutions. But neither cheap government nor the "true republic" was its ultimate aim; they were its mere concomitants.

The multiplicity of interpretations to which the Commune has been subjected, and the multiplicity of interests which construed it in their favour, show that it was a thoroughly expansive political form, while all previous forms of government had been emphatically repressive. Its true secret was this. It was essentially a working class government, the produce of the struggle of the producing against the appropriating class, the political form at last discovered under which to work out the economical emancipation of labour.[52]

Except on this last condition, the Communal Constitution would have been an impossibility and a delusion. The political rule of the producer cannot co-exist with the perpetuation of his social slavery. The Commune was therefore to serve as a lever for uprooting the economical foundations upon which rests the existence of classes, and therefore of class rule. With labour emancipated, every man becomes a working man, and productive labour ceases to be a class attribute.

It is a strange fact. In spite of all the tall talk and all the immense literature, for the last sixty years, about emancipation of labour, no sooner do the working men anywhere take the subject into their own hands with a will, than uprises at once all the apologetic phraseology of the mouthpieces of present society with its two poles of capital and wages-slavery (the landlord now is but the sleeping partner of the capitalist), as if capitalist society was still in its purest state of virgin innocence, with its antagonisms still undeveloped, with its delusions still unexploded, with its prostitute realities not yet laid bare. The Commune, they exclaim, intends to abolish property, the basis of all civilisation! Yes, gentlemen, the Commune intended to abolish that class property which makes the labour of the many the wealth of the few. It aimed at the expropriation of the expropriators. It wanted to make individual property a truth by transforming the means of production, land and capital, now chiefly the means of enslaving and exploiting labour, into mere instruments of free and associated labour. But this is communism, "impossible" communism! Why, those members of the ruling classes who are intelligent enough to perceive the impossibility of continuing the present system—and they are many—have become the obtrusive and full-mouthed apostles of co-operative production. If co-operative production is not to remain a sham and a snare; if it is to supersede the capitalist system; if united co-operative societies are to regulate national production upon a common plan, thus taking it under their own control, and putting an end to the constant anarchy and periodical convulsions which are the fatality of capitalist production—what else, gentlemen, would it be but communism, "possible" communism?

The working class did not expect miracles from the Commune. They have no ready-made utopias to introduce *par decret du peuple*. They know that in order to work out their own emancipation, and along with it that higher form to which present society is irresistibly tending by its own economical agencies, they will have to pass through long struggles, through a series of historic processes, transforming circumstances and men. They have no ideals to realise, but to set free the elements of the new society with which old collapsing bourgeois society itself is pregnant. In the full consciousness of their historic mission, and with the heroic resolve to act up to it, the working class can afford to smile at the coarse invective of the gentlemen's gentlemen with the pen and inkhorn, and at the didactic patronage of well-wishing bourgeois-doctrinaires, pouring forth their ignorant platitudes and sectarian crotchets in the oracular tone of scientific infallibility.

When the Paris Commune took the management of the revolution in its own hands; when plain working men for the first time dared to infringe upon the governmental privilege of their "natural superiors," and, under circumstances of unexampled difficulty, performed their work modestly, conscientiously, and efficiently—performed it at salaries the highest of which barely amounted to one-fifth of what, according to high scientific authority is the minimum required for a secretary to a certain metropolitan school-board—the old world writhed in convulsions of rage at the sight of the Red Flag, the symbol of the Republic of Labour, floating over the Hôtel de Ville.

And yet, this was the first revolution in which the working class was openly acknowledged as the only class capable of social initiative, even by the great bulk of the Paris middle class—shopkeepers, tradesmen, merchants—the wealthy capitalist alone excepted. The Commune had saved them [53] by a sagacious settlement of that ever recurring cause of dispute among the middle class themselves—the debtor and creditor accounts. The same portion of the middle class, after they had assisted in putting down the working men's insurrection of June 1848, had been at once unceremoniously sacrificed to their creditors by the then Constituent Assembly. But this was not their only motive for now rallying round the working class. They felt there was but one alternative—the Commune, or the empire—under whatever name it might reappear. The empire had ruined them economically by the havoc it made of public wealth, by the wholesale financial swindling it fostered, by the props it lent to the artificially accelerated centralisation of capital, and the con-comitant expropriation of their own ranks. It had suppressed them politically, it had shocked them morally by its orgies, it had insulted their Voltairianism [54] by handing over the education of their chil-dren to the *frères Ignorantins*, it had revolted their national feeling as Frenchmen by precipitating them headlong into a war which left only one equivalent for the ruins it made—the disappearance of the empire. In fact, after the exodus from Paris of the high Bonapartist and capitalist *bôhème*, the true middle class Party of Order came out in the shape of the *"Union Républicaine,"* enrolling themselves under the colours of the Commune and defending it against the wilful misconstruction of Thiers. Whether the gratitude of this great body of the middle class will stand the present severe trial, time must show.

The Commune was perfectly right in telling the peasants that "its victory was their only hope." Of all the lies hatched at Versailles and re-echoed by the glorious European penny-a-liner, one of the most tremendous was that the Rurals represented the French peas-antry. Think only of the love of the French peasant for the men to whom, after 1815, he had to pay the milliard of indemnity! [55] In the eyes of the French peasant, the very existence of a great landed proprietor is in itself an encroachment on his conquests of 1789. The bourgeois, in 1848, had burdened his plot of land with the additional tax of forty-five cents, [56] in the franc; but then he did so in the name of the revolution; while now he had fomented a civil war against the revolution, to shift on to the peasant's shoulders the chief load of the five milliards of indemnity to be paid to the Prussian. The Commune, on the other hand, in one of its first proclamations, declared that the true originators of the war would be made to pay its cost. The Commune would have delivered the peasant of the blood tax—would have given him a cheap gov-ernment—transformed his present blood-suckers, the notary, advo-cate, executor, and other judicial vampires, into salaried communal agents, elected by, and responsible to, himself. It would have freed him of the tyranny of the *garde champêtre*, the gendarme, and the prefect; would have put enlightenment by the schoolmaster in the place of stultification by the priest. And the French peasant is, above all, a man of reckoning. He would find it extremely reasonable that the pay of the priest, instead of being extorted by the tax-gatherer, should only depend upon the spontaneous action of the parishioners' religious instincts. Such were the great immediate boons which the rule of the Commune—and that rule alone—held out to the French peasantry. It is, therefore, quite superfluous here to expatiate upon the more complicated but vital problems which the Commune alone was able, and at the same time compelled, to solve in favour of the peasant, *viz.,* the hypothecary debt, lying like an incubus upon his parcel of soil, the *prolétariat foncier* (the rural proletariat), daily growing upon it, and his expropriation from it enforced, at a more and more rapid rate, by the very development of modern agriculture and the competition of capitalist farming.

The French peasant had elected Louis Bonaparte president of the republic; but the Party of Order [57] created the empire. What the French peasant really wants he commenced to show in 1849 and 1850, by opposing his *maire* to the government's prefect, his school-master to the government's priest, and himself to the government's gendarme. All the laws made by the Party of Order in January and February 1850 were avowed measures of repression against the peasant. The peasant was a Bonapartist, because the Great Revolution, with all its benefits to him, was, in his eyes, personified in Napoleon. This delusion, rapidly breaking down under the Second Empire (and in its very nature hostile to the Rurals), this prejudice of the past, how could it have withstood the appeal of the Commune to the living interests and urgent wants of the peasantry?

The Rurals—this was, in fact, their chief apprehension—knew that three months' free communication of Communal Paris with the provinces would bring about a general rising of the peasants, and hence their anxiety to establish a police blockade around Paris, so as to stop the spread of the rinderpest.

If the Commune was thus the true representative of all the healthy elements of French society, and therefore the truly national government, it was, at the same time, as a working men's government, as the bold champion of the emancipation of labour, emphatically international. Within sight of the Prussian army, that had annexed to Germany two French provinces,[58] the Commune annexed to France the working people all over the world.

The Second Empire had been the jubilee of cosmopolitan blackleggism, the rakes of all countries rushing in at its call for a share in its orgies and in the plunder of the French people. Even at this moment the right hand of Thiers is Ganessco, the foul Wallachian, and his left hand is Markovsky, the Russian spy. The Commune admitted all foreigners to the honour of dying for an immortal cause. Between the foreign war lost by their treason, and the civil war fomented by their conspiracy with the foreign invader, the bourgeoisie had found the time to display their patriotism by organising police hunts upon the Germans in France. The Commune made a German working man its Minister of Labour. Thiers, the bourgeoisie, the Second Empire, had continually deluded Poland by loud professions of sympathy, while in reality betraying her to, and doing the dirty work of, Russia. The Commune honoured the heroic sons of Poland by placing them at the head of the defenders of Paris. And, to broadly mark the new era of history it was conscious of initiating, under the eyes of the conquering Prussians on the one side, and of the Bonapartist army, led by Bonapartist generals, on the other, the Commune pulled down that colossal symbol of martial glory, the Vendôme Column.

The great social measure of the Commune was its own working existence. Its special measures could but betoken the tendency of a government of the people by the people. Such were the abolition of the nightwork of journeymen bakers; the prohibition, under penalty, of the employers' practice to reduce wages by levying upon their workpeople fines under manifold pretexts—a process in which the employer combines in his own person the parts of legislator, judge, and executor, and filches the money to boot. Another measure of this class was the surrender to associations of workmen, under reserve of compensation, of all closed workshops and factories, no matter whether the respective capitalists had absconded or preferred to strike work.

The financial measures of the Commune, remarkable for their

sagacity and moderation, could only be such as were compatible with the state of a besieged town. Considering the colossal robberies committed upon the city of Paris by the great financial companies and contractors, under the protection of Haussmann,[59] the Commune would have had an incomparably better title to confiscate their property than Louis Napoleon had against the Orleans family. The Hohenzollern and the English oligarchs, who both have derived a good deal of their estates from church plunder, were, of course, greatly shocked at the Commune clearing but 8,000 *f.* out of secularisation.

While the Versailles government, as soon as it had recovered some spirit and strength, used the most violent means against the Commune; while it put down the free expression of opinion all over France, even to the forbidding of meetings of delegates from the large towns; while it subjected Versailles and the rest of France to an espionage far surpassing that of the Second Empire; while it burned by its gendarme inquisitors all papers printed at Paris, and sifted all correspondence from and to Paris; while in the National Assembly the most timid attempts to put in a word for Paris were howled down in a manner unknown even to the *Chambre introuvable* of 1816; with the savage warfare of Versailles outside, and its attempts at corruption and conspiracy inside Paris— would the Commune not have shamefully betrayed its trust by affecting to keep up all the decencies and appearances of liberalism as in a time of profound peace? Had the government of the Commune been akin to that of M. Thiers, there would have been no more occasion to suppress Party of Order papers at Paris than there was to suppress Communal papers at Versailles.

It was irritating indeed to the Rurals that at the very same time they declared the return to the church to be the only means of salvation for France, the infidel Commune unearthed the peculiar mysteries of the Picpus nunnery, and of the Church of St. Laurent.[60] It was a satire upon M. Thiers that, while he showered grand crosses upon the Bonapartist generals in acknowledgment of their mastery in losing battles, signing capitulations, and turning cigarettes at Wilhelmshöhe, the Commune dismissed and arrested its generals whenever they were suspected of neglecting their duties. The expulsion from, and arrest by, the Commune of one of its members who had slipped in under a false name, and had undergone at Lyons six days' imprisonment for simple bankruptcy, was it not a deliberate insult hurled at the forger, Jules Favre, then still the foreign minister of France, still selling France to Bismarck, and still dictating his orders to that paragon government of Belgium? But indeed the Commune did not pretend to infallibility, the invariable attribute of all governments of the old stamp. It published its doings and sayings, it initiated the public into all its shortcomings.

In every revolution there intrude, at the side of its true agents, men of a different stamp; some of them survivors of and devotees to past revolutions, without insight into the present movement, but preserving popular influence by their known honesty and courage, or by the sheer force of tradition; others mere brawlers, who, by dint of repeating year after year the same set of stereotyped declamations against the government of the day, have sneaked into the reputation of revolutionists of the first water. After the 18th of March, some such men did also turn up, and in some cases contrived to play pre-eminent parts. As far as their power went, they hampered the real action of the working class, exactly as men of that sort have hampered the full development of every previous revolution. They are an unavoidable evil: with time they are shaken off; but time was not allowed to the Commune.

Wonderful, indeed, was the change the Commune had wrought in Paris! No longer any trace of the meretricious Paris of the Second Empire! No longer was Paris the rendezvous of British landlords, Irish absentees,[61] American ex-slaveholders and shoddy men, Russian ex-serfowners, and Wallachian boyards. No more corpses at the morgue, no nocturnal burglaries, scarcely any robberies; in fact, for the first time since the days of February 1848, the streets of Paris were safe, and that without any police of any kind. "We," said a member of the Commune, "hear no longer of assassination, theft and personal assault; it seems indeed as if the police had dragged along with it to Versailles all its Conservative friends." The *cocottes* had refound the scent of their protectors—the absconding men of family, religion, and, above all, of property. In their stead, the real women of Paris showed again at the surface—heroic, noble, and devoted, like the women of antiquity. Working, thinking, fighting, bleeding Paris—almost forgetful, in its incubation of a new society, of the cannibals at its gates—radiant in the enthusiasm of its historic initiative!

Opposed to this new world at Paris, behold the old world at Versailles—that assembly of the ghouls of all defunct *régimes*, Legitimists and Orleanists, eager to feed upon the carcass of the nation—with a tail of antediluvian republicans, sanctioning, by their presence in the Assembly, the slaveholders' rebellion, relying for the maintenance of their parliamentary republic upon the vanity of the senile mountebank at its head, and caricaturing 1789 by holding their ghastly meetings in the *Jeu de Paume*.[62] There it was, this Assembly, the representative of everything dead in France, propped up to the semblance of life by nothing but the swords of the generals of Louis Bonaparte. Paris all truth, Versailles all lie; and that lie vented through the mouth of Thiers.

Thiers tells a deputation of the mayors of the Seine-et-Oise—"You may rely upon my word, which I have *never* broken!" He tells the Assembly itself that "it was the most freely elected and most liberal Assembly France ever possessed"; he tells his motley soldiery that it was "the admiration of the world, and the finest army France ever possessed"; he tells the provinces that the bombardment of Paris by him was a myth: "If some cannon-shots have been fired, it is not the deed of the army of Versailles, but of some insurgents trying to make believe that they are fighting, while they dare not show their faces." He again tells the provinces that "the artillery of Versailles does not bombard Paris, but only cannonades it." He tells the Archbishop of Paris that the pretended executions and reprisals (!) attributed to the Versailles troops were all moonshine. He tells Paris that he was only anxious "to free it from the hideous tyrants who oppress it," and that, in fact, the Paris of the Commune was "but a handful of criminals."

The Paris of M. Thiers was not the real Paris of the "vile

multitude," but a phantom Paris, the Paris of the *francs-fileurs,* the
Paris of the Boulevards, male and female—the rich, the capitalist,
the gilded, the idle Paris, now thronging with its lackeys, its black-
legs, its literary *bôhème,* and its *cocottes* at Versailles, Saint-Denis,
Rueil, and Saint-Germain; considering the civil war but an agree-
able diversion, eyeing the battle going on through telescopes, count-
ing the rounds of cannon, and swearing by their own honour and
that of their prostitutes, that the performance was far better got
up than it used to be at the Porte St. Martin. The men who fell
were really dead; the cries of the wounded were cries in good
earnest; and, besides, the whole thing was so intensely historical.

   This is the Paris of M. Thiers, as the emigration of Coblenz [63]
was the France of M. de Calonne. [64]

IV

   The first attempt of the slaveholders' conspiracy to put down
Paris by getting the Prussians to occupy it was frustrated by Bismarck's refusal. The second attempt, that of the 18th of March,
ended in the rout of the army and the flight to Versailles of the
government, which ordered the whole administration to break up
and follow in its track. By the semblance of peace negotiations
with Paris, Thiers found the time to prepare for war against it.
But where to find an army? The remnants of the line regiments
were weak in number and unsafe in character. His urgent appeal
to the provinces to succour Versailles, by their National Guards
and volunteers, met with a flat refusal. Brittany alone furnished
a handful of *Chouans* fighting under a white flag, every one of
them wearing on his breast the heart of Jesus in white cloth, and
shouting *"Vive le Roi!"* (Long live the King!) Thiers was, therefore, compelled to collect, in hot haste, a motley crew, composed
of sailors, marines, Pontifical Zouaves, Valentin's gendarmes, and
Pietri's *sergents-de-ville* and *mouchards.* This army, however, would
have been ridiculously ineffective without the instalments of imperialist war prisoners, which Bismarck granted in numbers just
sufficient to keep the civil war agoing, and keep the Versailles

government in abject dependence on Prussia. During the war itself, the Versailles police had to look after the Versailles army, while the gendarmes had to drag it on by exposing themselves at all posts of danger. The forts which fell were not taken, but bought. The heroism of the Federals convinced Thiers that the resistance of Paris was not to be broken by his own strategic genius and the bayonets at his disposal.

Meanwhile, his relations with the provinces became more and more difficult. Not one single address of approval came in to gladden Thiers and his Rurals. Quite the contrary. Deputations and addresses demanding, in a tone anything but respectful, conciliation with Paris on the basis of the unequivocal recognition of the re-public, the acknowledgment of the Communal liberties, and the dissolution of the National Assembly, whose mandate was extinct, poured in from all sides, and in such numbers that Dufaure, Thiers' Minister of Justice, in his circular of April 23 to the public prosecutors, commanded them to treat "the cry of conciliation" as a crime! In regard, however, of the hopeless prospect held out by his campaign, Thiers resolved to shift his tactics by ordering, all over the country, municipal elections to take place on the 30th of April, on the basis of the new municipal law dictated by himself to the National Assembly. What with the intrigues of his prefects, what with police intimidation, he felt quite sanguine of imparting, by the verdict of the provinces, to the National Assembly that moral power it had never possessed, and of getting at last from the provinces the physical force required for the conquest of Paris.

His banditti-warfare against Paris, exalted in his own bulletins, and the attempts of his ministers at the establishment, throughout France, of a reign of terror, Thiers was from the beginning anxious to accompany with a little by-play of conciliation, which had to serve more than one purpose. It was to dupe the provinces, to inveigle the middle class element in Paris, and, above all, to afford the professed republicans in the National Assembly the opportunity of hiding their treason against Paris behind their faith in Thiers. On the 21st of March, when still without an army, he had declared to the Assembly: "Come what may, I will not send an army to

Paris." On the 27th March he rose again: "I have found the republic an accomplished fact, and I am firmly resolved to maintain it." In reality, he put down the revolution at Lyons and Marseilles[65] in the name of the republic, while the roars of his Rurals drowned the very mention of its name at Versailles. After this exploit, he toned down the "accomplished fact" into an hypothetical fact. The Orleans princes, whom he had cautiously warned off Bordeaux, were now, in flagrant breach of the law, permitted to intrigue at Dreux. The concessions held out by Thiers in his interminable interviews with the delegates from Paris and the provinces, although constantly varied in tone and colour, according to time and circumstances, did in fact never come to more than the prospective restriction of revenge to the "handful of criminals implicated in the murder of Lecomte and Clement Thomas," on the well-understood premise that Paris and France were unreservedly to accept M. Thiers himself as the best of possible Republics, as he, in 1830, had done with Louis Philippe. Even these concessions he not only took care to render doubtful by the official comments put upon them in the Assembly through his ministers. He had his Dufaure to act. Dufaure, this old Orleanist lawyer, had always been the justiciary of the state of siege, as now in 1871, under Thiers, so in 1839 under Louis Philippe, and in 1849 under Louis Bonaparte's presidency. While out of office he made a fortune by pleading for the Paris capitalists, and made political capital by pleading against the laws he had himself originated. He now hurried through the National Assembly not only a set of repressive laws which were, after the fall of Paris, to extirpate the last remnants of republican liberty in France; he foreshadowed the fate of Paris by abridging the, for him, too slow procedure of courts-martial, and by a new-fangled, Draconic code of deportation. The Revolution of 1848, abolishing the penalty of death for political crimes, had replaced it by deportation. Louis Bonaparte did not dare, at least not in theory, to re-establish the regime of the guillotine. The Rural Assembly, not yet bold enough even to hint that the Parisians were not rebels, but assassins, had therefore to confine its prospective vengeance against Paris to Dufaure's new code of deportation. Under all these circumstances Thiers himself could not have gone on with his comedy of conciliation, had it not, as he intended it to do, drawn forth shrieks of rage from the Rurals, whose ruminating mind did neither understand the play, nor its necessities of hypocrisy, tergiversation, and procrastination.

In sight of the impending municipal elections of the 30th April, Thiers enacted one of his great conciliation scenes on the 27th April. Amidst a flood of sentimental rhetoric, he exclaimed from the tribune of the Assembly:

"There exists no conspiracy against the republic but that of Paris, which compels us to shed French blood. I repeat it again and again. Let those impious arms fall from the hands which hold them, and chastisement will be arrested at once by an act of peace excluding only the small number of criminals."

To the violent interruption of the Rurals he replied:

"Gentlemen, tell me, I implore you, am I wrong? Do you really regret that I could have stated the truth that the criminals are only a handful? Is it not fortunate in the midst of our misfortunes that those who have been capable to shed the blood of Clement Thomas and General Lecomte are but rare exceptions?"

France, however, turned a deaf ear to what Thiers flattered himself to be a parliamentary siren's song. Out of 700,000 municipal councillors returned by the 35,000 communes still left to France, the united Legitimists, Orleanists, and Bonapartists did not carry 8,000. The supplementary elections which followed were still more decidedly hostile. Thus, instead of getting from the provinces the badly-needed physical force, the National Assembly lost even its last claim to moral force, that of being the expression of the universal suffrage of the country. To complete the discomfiture, the newly-chosen municipal councils of all the cities of France openly threatened the usurping Assembly at Versailles with a counter assembly at Bordeaux.

Then the long-expected moment of decisive action had at last come for Bismarck. He peremptorily summoned Thiers to send to Frankfort plenipotentiaries for the definitive settlement of peace. In humble obedience to the call of his master, Thiers hastened to despatch his trusty Jules Favre, backed by Pouyer-Quertier. Pouyer-Quertier, an "eminent" Rouen cotton-spinner, a fervent and even servile partisan of the Second Empire, had never found any fault with it save its commercial treaty with England,[66] prejudicial to his own shop-interest. Hardly installed at Bordeaux as Thiers' Minister of Finance, he denounced that "unholy" treaty, hinted at its near abrogation, and had even the effrontery to try, although in vain (having counted without Bismarck), the immediate enforcement of the old protective duties against Alsace, where, he said, no previous international treaties stood in the way. This man who considered counter-revolution as a means to put down wages at Rouen, and the surrender of French provinces as a means to bring up the price of his wares in France, was he not *the one* predestined to be picked out by Thiers as the helpmate of Jules Favre in his last and crowning treason?

On the arrival at Frankfort of this exquisite pair of plenipotentiaries, bully Bismarck at once met them with the imperious alternative: Either the restoration of the empire or the unconditional acceptance of my own peace terms! These terms included a shortening of the intervals in which the war indemnity was to be paid and the continued occupation of the Paris forts by Prussian troops until Bismarck should feel satisfied with the state of things in France; Prussia thus being recognised as the supreme arbiter in internal French politics! In return for this he offered to let loose, for the extermination of Paris, the captive Bonapartist army, and to lend them the direct assistance of Emperor William's troops. He pledged his good faith by making payment of the first instalment of the indemnity dependent on the "pacification" of Paris. Such a bait was, of course, eagerly swallowed by Thiers and his plenipotentiaries. They signed the treaty of peace on the 10th of May and had it endorsed by the Versailles Assembly on the 18th.

In the interval between the conclusion of peace and the arrival of the Bonapartist prisoners, Thiers felt the more bound to resume his comedy of conciliation, as his republican tools stood in sore need of a pretext for blinking their eyes at the preparations for the carnage of Paris. As late as the 8th May he replied to a deputation of middle class conciliators—

"Whenever the insurgents will make up their minds for capitulation, the gates of Paris shall be flung wide open during a week for all except the murderers of Generals Clement Thomas and Lecomte."

A few days afterwards, when violently interpellated on these promises by the Rurals, he refused to enter into any explanations; not, however, without giving them this significant hint:

"I tell you there are impatient men amongst you, men who are in too great a hurry. They must have another eight days; at the end of these eight days there will be no more danger, and the task will be proportionate to their courage and to their capacities."

As soon as MacMahon was able to assure him that he could shortly enter Paris, Thiers declared to the Assembly that "he would enter Paris with the *laws* in his hands, and demand a full expiation from the wretches who had sacrificed the lives of soldiers and destroyed public monuments." As the moment of decision drew near he said—to the Assembly, "I shall be pitiless!"—to Paris, that it was doomed; and to his Bonapartist banditti, that they had state licence to wreak vengeance upon Paris to their hearts' content. At last, when treachery had opened the gates of Paris to General Douai, on the 21st May, Thiers, on the 22nd, revealed to the Rurals the "goal" of his conciliation comedy, which they had so obstinately persisted in not understanding. "I told you a few days ago that we were approaching *our goal;* today I come to tell you *the* goal is reached. The victory of order, justice and civilisation is at last won!"

So it was. The civilisation and justice of bourgeois order comes out in its lurid light whenever the slaves and drudges of that order rise against their masters. Then this civilisation and justice stand forth as undisguised savagery and lawless revenge. Each new crisis in the class struggle between the appropriator and the producer brings out this fact more glaringly. Even the atrocities of the bourgeois in June 1848 vanish before the ineffable infamy of 1871. The self-sacrificing heroism with which the population of Paris—men, women and children—fought for eight days after the entrance of the Versaillese, reflects as much the grandeur of their cause, as the infernal deeds of the soldiery reflect the innate spirit of that civilisation of which they are the mercenary vindicators. A glorious civilisation, indeed, the great problem of which is how to get rid of the heaps of corpses it made after the battle was over!

To find a parallel for the conduct of Thiers and his bloodhounds we must go back to the times of Sulla and the two Triumvirates of Rome. The same wholesale slaughter in cold blood; the same disregard, in massacre, of age and sex, the same system of torturing prisoners; the same proscriptions, but this time of a whole class; the same savage hunt after concealed leaders, lest one might escape; the same denunciations of political and private enemies; the same indifference for the butchery of entire strangers to the feud. There is but this difference, that the Romans had no *mitrailleuses* for the despatch, in the lump, of the proscribed, and that they had not "the law in their hands," nor on their lips the cry of "civilisation."

And after those horrors look upon the other still more hideous face of that bourgeois civilisation as described by its own press!

"With stray shots," writes the Paris correspondent of a London Tory paper, "still ringing in the distance, and untended wounded wretches dying amid the tombstones of Père la Chaise—with 6,000 terror-stricken insurgents wandering in an agony of despair in the labyrinth of the catacombs, and wretches hurried through the streets to be shot down in scores by the *mitrailleuse*—it is revolting to see the *cafés* filled with the votaries of absinthe, billiards and dominoes; female profligacy perambulating the boulevards, and the sound of revelry disturbing the night from the *cabinets particuliers* of fashionable restaurants."

M. Edouard Hervé writes in the *Journal de Paris*, a Versaillist journal pressed by the Commune:

"The way in which the population of Paris [!] manifested its satisfaction yesterday was rather more than frivolous, and we fear it will grow worse as time progresses. Paris has now a *fête* day appearance, which is sadly out of place; and, unless we are to be called the *Parisiens de la décadence,* this sort of thing must come to an end."

And then he quotes the passage from Tacitus:

"Yet, on the morrow of that horrible struggle, even before it was completely over, Rome—degraded and corrupt—began once more to wallow in the voluptuous slough which was destroying its body and polluting its soul—*alibi prœlia et vulnera, alibi balnea popinœque* [here fights and wounds, there baths and restaurants]."

M. Hervé only forgets to say that the "population of Paris" he speaks of is but the population of the Paris of M. Thiers—the *francs-fileurs* returning in throngs from Versailles, Saint-Denis, Rueil, and Saint Germain—*the* Paris of the "Decline."

In all its bloody triumphs over the self-sacrificing champions of a new and better society, that nefarious civilisation, based upon the enslavement of labour, drowns the moans of its victims in a hue-and-cry of calumny, reverberated by a world-wide echo. The serene working men's Paris of the Commune is suddenly changed into a pandemonium by the bloodhounds of "order." And what does this tremendous change prove to the bourgeois mind of all countries? Why, that the Commune has conspired against civilisation! The Paris people die enthusiastically for the Commune in numbers un-equalled in any battle known to history. What does that prove? Why, that the Commune was not the people's own government but the usurpation of a handful of criminals! The women of Paris joy-fully give up their lives at the barricades and on the place of execution. What does this prove? Why, that the demon of the Commune has changed them into Megæras and Hecates! The mod-eration of the Commune during two months of undisputed sway is equalled only by the heroism of its defence. What does that prove? Why, that for months the Commune carefully hid, under a mask of moderation and humanity, the bloodthirstiness of its fiend-ish instincts, to be let loose in the hour of its agony!

The working men's Paris, in the act of its heroic self-holocaust, involved in its flames buildings and monuments. While tearing to pieces the living body of the proletariat, its rulers must no longer expect to return triumphantly into the intact architecture of their abodes. The government of Versailles cries, "Incendiarism!" and whispers this cue to all its agents, down to the remotest hamlet, to hunt up its enemies everywhere as suspect of professional incendiarism. The bourgeoisie of the whole world, which looks complacently upon the wholesale massacre after the battle, is convulsed by horror at the desecration of brick and mortar!

When governments give state licences to their navies to "kill, *burn,* and destroy," is that a licence for incendiarism? When the British troops wantonly set fire to the Capitol at Washington and to the summer palace of the Chinese emperor, was that incendiarism? When the Prussians not for military reasons, but out of the mere spite of revenge, burned down, by the help of petroleum, towns like Chateâudun and innumerable villages, was that incendiarism? When Thiers, during six weeks, bombarded Paris, under the pretext that he wanted to set fire to those houses only in which there were people, was that incendiarism?—In war, fire is an arm as legitimate as any. Buildings held by the enemy are shelled to set them on fire. If their defenders have to retire, they themselves light the flames to prevent the attack from making use of the buildings. To be burned down has always been the inevitable fate of all buildings situated in the front of battle of all the regular armies of the world. But in the war of the enslaved against their enslavers, the only justifiable war in history, this is by no means to hold good! The Commune used fire strictly as a means of defence. They used it to stop up to the Versailles troops those long, straight avenues which Haussmann had expressly opened to artillery-fire; they used it to cover their retreat, in the same way as the Versaillese, in their advance, used their shells which destroyed at least as many buildings as the fire of the Commune. It is a matter of dispute, even now, which buildings were set fire to by the defence, and which by the attack. And the defence resorted to fire only then when the Versaillese troops had already commenced their wholesale murdering of prisoners.—Besides, the Commune had, long before, given full public notice that if driven to extremities, they would bury themselves under the ruins of Paris, and make Paris a second Moscow, as the Government of Defence, but only as a cloak for its treason, had promised to do. For this purpose Trochu had found them the petroleum. The Commune knew that its opponents cared nothing for the lives of the Paris people, but cared much for their own Paris buildings. And Thiers, on the other hand, had given them notice that he would be implacable in his vengeance. No sooner had he got his army ready on one side, and the Prussians shutting up the trap on the other, than he proclaimed: "I shall be pitiless! The expiation will be complete, and justice will be stern!" If the acts of the Paris working men were vandalism, it was the vandalism of defence in despair, not the vandalism of triumph, like that which the Christians perpetrated upon the really priceless art treasures of heathen antiquity; and even that vandalism has been justified by the historian as an unavoidable and comparatively trifling concomitant to the titanic struggle between a new society arising and an old one breaking down. It was still less the vandalism of Haussmann, razing historic Paris to make place for the Paris of the sightseer!

But the execution by the Commune of the sixty-four hostages, with the Archbishop of Paris at their head! The bourgeoisie and its army in June 1848 re-established a custom which had long disappeared from the practice of war—the shooting of their defenceless prisoners. This brutal custom has since been more or less strictly adhered to by the suppressors of all popular commotions in Europe and India; thus proving that it constitutes a real "progress of civilisation"! On the other hand, the Prussians, in France, had re-established the practice of taking hostages—innocent men, who, with their lives, were to answer to them for the acts of others. When Thiers, as we have seen, from the very beginning of the conflict, enforced the humane practice of shooting down the Communal prisoners, the Commune, to protect their lives, was obliged to resort to the Prussian practice of securing hostages. The lives of the hostages have been forfeited over and over again by the continued shooting of prisoners on the part of the Versaillese. How could they be spared any longer after the carnage with which Mac-Mahon's prætorians celebrated their entrance into Paris? Was even the last check upon the unscrupulous ferocity of bourgeois governments—the taking of hostages—to be made a mere sham of? The real murderer of Archbishop Darboy is Thiers. The Commune again and again had offered to exchange the archbishop, and ever so many priests in the bargain, against the single Blanqui, then in the hands of Thiers. Thiers obstinately refused. He knew that with Blanqui he would give to the Commune a head; while the archbishop would serve his purpose best in the shape of a corpse. Thiers acted upon the precedent of Cavaignac. How, in June 1848, did not Cavaignac and his men of order raise shouts of horror by stigmatising the insurgents as the assassins of Archbishop Affre! They knew perfectly well that the archbishop had been shot by the soldiers of order. M. Jacquemet, the archbishop's vicar-general, present on the spot, had immediately afterwards handed them in his evidence to that effect.

All this chorus of calumny, which the Party of Order never fail, in their orgies of blood, to raise against their victims, only proves that the bourgeois of our days considers himself the legitimate successor to the baron of old, who thought every weapon in his own hand fair against the plebeian, while in the hands of the plebeian a weapon of any kind constituted in itself a crime.

The conspiracy of the ruling class to break down the revolution by a civil war carried on under the patronage of the foreign invader—a conspiracy which we have traced from the very 4th of September down to the entrance of MacMahon's prætorians through the gate of St. Cloud—culminated in the carnage of Paris. Bismarck gloats over the ruins of Paris, in which he saw perhaps the first instalment of that general destruction of great cities he had prayed for when still a simple Rural in the Prussian *Chambre introuvable* of 1849. He gloats over the cadavres of the Paris proletariat. For him this is not only the extermination of revolution, but the extinction of France, now decapitated in reality, and by the French government itself. With the shallowness characteristic of all successful statesmen, he sees but the surface of this tremendous historic event. Whenever before has history exhibited the spectacle of a conqueror crowning his victory by turning into, not only the gendarme, but the hired bravo of the conquered government? There existed no war between Prussia and the Commune of Paris. On the contrary, the Commune had accepted the peace preliminaries, and Prussia had announced her neutrality. Prussia was, therefore, no belligerent. She acted the part of a bravo, a cowardly bravo, because incurring no danger; a hired bravo, because stipulating beforehand the payment of her blood-money of 500 millions on the fall of Paris. And thus, at last, came out the true character of the war, ordained by Providence as a chastisement of godless and debauched France by pious and moral Germany! And this unparalleled breach of the law of nations, even as understood by the old-world lawyers, instead of arousing the "civilised" governments of Europe to declare the felonious Prussian government, the mere tool of the St. Petersburg Cabinet, an outlaw amongst nations, only incites them to consider whether the few victims who escape the double cordon around Paris are not to be given up to the hangman of Versailles!

That after the most tremendous war of modern times, the conquering and the conquered hosts should fraternise for the common massacre of the proletariat—this unparalleled event does indicate, not, as Bismarck thinks, the final repression of a new society upheaving, but the crumbling into dust of bourgeois society. The highest heroic effort of which old society is still capable is national war; and this is now proved to be a mere governmental humbug, intended to defer the struggle of classes, and to be thrown aside as soon as that class struggle bursts out into civil war. Class rule is no longer able to disguise itself in a national uniform; the national governments are *one* as against the proletariat!

After Whit-Sunday, 1871, there can be neither peace nor truce possible between the working men of France and the appropriators of their produce. The iron hand of a mercenary soldiery may keep for a time both classes tied down in common oppression. But the battle must break out again and again in ever-growing dimensions, and there can be no doubt as to who will be the victor in the end—the appropriating few, or the immense working majority. And the

French working class is only the advanced guard of the modern proletariat.

While the European governments thus testify, before Paris, to the international character of class rule, they cry down the International Working Men's Association—the international counter-organisation of labour against the cosmopolitan conspiracy of capital —as the head fountain of all these disasters. Thiers denounced it as the despot of labour, pretending to be its liberator. Picard ordered that all communications between the French Internationals and those abroad should be cut off; Count Jaubert, Thiers' mummified accomplice of 1835, declares it the great problem of all civilised governments to weed it out. The Rurals roar against it, and the whole European press joins the chorus. An honourable French writer, completely foreign to our Association, speaks as follows:

"The members of the Central Committee of the National Guard, as well as the greater part of the members of the Commune, are the most active, intelligent, and energetic minds of the International Working Men's Association ... men who are thoroughly honest, sincere, intelligent, devoted, pure, and fanatical in the *good* sense of the word."

The police-tinged bourgeois mind naturally figures to itself the International Working Men's Association as acting in the manner of a secret conspiracy, its central body ordering, from time to time, explosions in different countries. Our Association is, in fact, nothing but the international bond between the most advanced working men in the various countries of the civilised world. Wherever, in whatever shape, and under whatever conditions the class struggle obtains any consistency, it is but natural that members of our Association should stand in the foreground. The soil out of which it grows is modern society itself. It cannot be stamped out by any amount of carnage. To stamp it out, the governments would have to stamp out the despotism of capital over labour—the condition of their own parasitical existence.

Working men's Paris, with its Commune, will be for ever celebrated as the glorious harbinger of a new society. Its martyrs are enshrined in the great heart of the working class. Its exterminators history has already nailed to that eternal pillory from which all the prayers of their priest will not avail to redeem them.

THE GENERAL COUNCIL

M. J. BOON, FRED. BRADNICK, G. H. BUTTERY, CAIHIL, DELAHAYE, WILLIAM HALES, A. HERMANN, KOLB, FRED. LESSNER, LOCHNER, T. P. MACDONNELL, GEORGE MILNER, THOMAS MOTTERSHEAD, CH. MILLS, CHARLES MURRAY, PFANDER, ROACH, ROCHAT, RUHL, SADLER, A. SERRAILLIER, COWELL STEPNEY, ALF. TAYLOR, WILLIAM TOWNSHEND.

CORRESPONDING SECRETARIES

EUGENE DUPONT, *for France*
KARL MARX, *for Germany and Holland*
FRED. ENGELS, *for Belgium and Spain*
HERMANN JUNG, *for Switzerland*
P. GIOVACCHINI, *for Italy*

ZEVY MAURICE, *for Hungary*
ANTON ZABICKI, *for Poland*
JAMES COHEN, *for Denmark*
J. G. ECCARIUS, *for the United States*

HERMANN JUNG, *Chairman*
JOHN WESTON, *Treasurer*
GEORGE HARRIS, *Financial Secretary*
JOHN HALES, *General Secretary*

Office: 256 High Holborn, London, W.C., *May 30, 1871*

"The column of prisoners halted in the Avenue Uhrich, and was drawn up, four or five deep, on the footway facing to the road. General Marquis de Gallifet and his staff dismounted and commenced an inspection from the left of the line. Walking down slowly and eyeing the ranks, the general stopped here and there, tapping a man on the shoulder or beckoning him out of the rear ranks. In most cases, without further parley, the individual thus selected was marched out into the centre of the road, where a small supplementary column was thus soon formed.... It was evident that there was considerable room for error. A mounted officer pointed out to General Gallifet a man and woman for some particular offence. The woman, rushing out of the ranks, threw herself on her knees, and, with outstretched arms, protested her innocence in passionate terms. The general waited for a pause, and then with most impassible face and unmoved demeanour, said: 'Madame, I have visited every theatre in Paris, your acting will have no effect on me' ('ce n'est pas la peine de jouer la comedie').... It was not a good thing on that day to be noticeably taller, dirtier, cleaner, older, or uglier than one's neighbours. One individual in particular struck me as probably owing his speedy release from the ills of this world to his having a broken nose.... Over a hundred being thus chosen, a firing party told off, and the column resumed its march, leaving them behind. A few minutes afterwards a dropping fire in our rear commenced, and continued for over a quarter of an hour. It was the execution of the summarily-convicted wretches." —Paris Correspondent *Daily News,* June 8.—This Gallifet, "the kept man of his wife, so notorious for her shameless exhibitions at the orgies of the Second Empire," went, during the war, by the name of the French "Ensign Pistol."

"The *Temps,* which is a careful journal, and not given to sensation, tells a dreadful story of people imperfectly shot and buried before life was extinct. A great number were buried in the Square round St. Jacques-la-Bouchière; some of them very superficially. In the daytime the roar of the busy streets prevented any notice being taken; but in the stillness of the night the inhabitants of the houses in the neighbourhood were roused by distant moans, and in the morning a clenched hand was seen protruding through the soil. In consequence of this, exhumations were ordered to take place.... That many wounded have been buried alive I have not the slightest doubt. One case I can vouch for. When Brunel was shot with his mistress on the 24th ult. in the courtyard of a house in the Place Vendôme, the bodies lay there until the afternoon of the 27th. When the burial party came to remove the corpses, they found the woman living still, and took her to an ambulance. Though she had received four bullets she is now out of danger."—Paris Correspondent *Evening Standard,* June 8.

II

The following letter appeared in the [London] *Times,* June 13th:

"To the Editor of the *Times:*

"Sir,—On June 6, 1871, M. Jules Favre[71] issued a circular to all the European Powers, calling upon them to hunt down the International Working Men's Association. A few remarks will suffice to characterize that document.

"In the very preamble of our statutes it is stated that the International was founded 'September 28, 1864, at a public meeting held at St. Martin's Hall, Long Acre, London.' For purposes of his own Jules Favre puts back the date of its origin behind 1862.

"In order to explain our principles, he professes to quote 'their (the International's) sheet of the 25th of March, 1869.' And then what does he quote? The sheet of a society which is not the International. This sort of a manoeuvre he already recurred to when, still a comparatively young lawyer, he had to defend the *National* newspaper, prosecuted for libel by Cabet.[72] Then he pretended to read extracts from Cabet's pamphlets while reading interpolations of his own—a trick exposed while the court was sitting, and which, but for the indulgence of Cabet, would have been punished by Jules Favre's expulsion from the Paris bar. Of all the documents quoted by him as documents of the International, not one belongs to the International. He says, for instance, 'The Alliance declares itself Atheist, says the General Council, constituted in London in July 1869.' The General Council never issued such a document. On the contrary, it issued a document which quashed the original statutes of the 'Alliance'—L'Alliance de la Démocratie Socialiste at Geneva —quoted by Jules Favre.

"Throughout his circular, which pretends in part also to be directed against the Empire, Jules Favre repeats against the International but the police inventions of the public prosecutors of the Empire, which broke down miserably even before the law courts of that Empire.

"It is known that in its two Addresses (of July and September last) on the late war, the General Council of the International denounced the Prussian plans of conquest against France. Later on, Mr. Reitlinger, Jules Favre's private secretary, applied, though of course in vain, to some members of the General Council for getting up by the Council a demonstration against Bismarck, in favour of the Government of National Defence; they were particularly requested not to mention the republic. The preparations for a demonstration with regard to the expected arrival of Jules Favre in London were made—certainly with the best of intentions—in spite of the General Council, which, in its address of the 9th of September, had distinctly forewarned the Paris workmen against Jules Favre and his colleagues.

"What would Jules Favre say if, in its turn, the International were to send a circular on Jules Favre to all the Cabinets of Europe, drawing their particular attention to the documents published at Paris by the late M. Millière?[73]

"I am, Sir, your obedient servant,

"*John Hales,* Secretary to the General Council of the International Working Men's Association. London, *June 12th, 1871.*"[74]

IV

LETTERS TO DR. KUGELMANN ON THE PARIS COMMUNE [67]

April 12, 1871

...IF YOU look at the last chapter of my *Eighteenth Brumaire* you will find that I say that the next attempt of the French revolution will be no longer, as before, to transfer the bureaucratic-military machine from one hand to another, but to *smash* it, and this is essential for every real people's revolution on the Continent.[68] And this is what our heroic Party comrades in Paris are attempting. What elasticity, what historical initiative, what a capacity for sacrifice in these Parisians! After six months of hunger and ruin, caused rather by internal treachery than by the external enemy, they rise, beneath Prussian bayonets, as if there had never been a war between France and Germany and the enemy were not at the gates of Paris. History has no like example of a like greatness. If they are defeated only their "good nature" will be to blame. They should have marched at once on Versailles, after first Vinoy and then the reactionary section of the Paris National Guard had themselves retreated. The right moment was missed because of conscientious scruples. They did not want to *start the civil war,* as if that mischievous *abortion* Thiers had not already started the civil war with his attempt to disarm Paris. Second mistake: The Central Committee surrendered its power too soon, to make way for the Commune. Again from a too "honourable" scrupulosity! [69] However that may be, the present rising in Paris—even if it be crushed by the wolves, swine and vile curs of the old society—is the most glorious deed of our Party since the June insurrection in Paris. Compare these Parisians, storming heaven, with the slaves to heaven of the German-Prussian Holy Roman Empire, with its posthumous masquerades reeking of the barracks, the Church, cabbage-*junkerdom* and above all, of the philistine.

A propos. In the *official publication* of the list of those receiving direct subsidies from Louis Bonaparte's treasury there is a note that Vogt received 40,000 francs in August 1859. I have informed Liebknecht of the *fait*, for further use.

[London] April 17, 1871

...How you can compare petty-bourgeois demonstrations *à la* 13 June, 1849,[70] etc., with the present struggle in Paris is quite incomprehensible to me.

World history would indeed be very easy to make, if the struggle were taken up only on condition of infallibly favourable chances. It would, on the other hand, be of a very mystical nature, if "accidents" played no part. These accidents themselves fall naturally into the general course of development and are compensated again by other accidents. But acceleration and delay are very dependent upon such "accidents," which include the "accident" of the character of those who at first stand at the head of the movement.

The decisive, unfavourable "accident" this time is by no means to be found in the general conditions of French society, but in the presence of the Prussians in France and their position right before Paris. Of this the Parisians were well aware. But of this, the bourgeois *canaille* of Versailles were also well aware. Precisely for that reason they presented the Parisians with the alternative of taking up the fight or succumbing without a struggle. In the latter case, the demoralisation of the working class would have been a far greater misfortune than the fall of any number of "leaders." The struggle of the working class against the capitalist class and its state has entered upon a new phase with the struggle in Paris. Whatever the immediate results may be, a new point of departure of world-historic importance has been gained.

PART TWO

WRITINGS ON THE COMMUNE
by V. I. Lenin

MARX'S ASSESSMENT of the Commune crowns the letters to Kugelmann. And this assessment is particularly valuable when compared with the methods of the Russian Right-wing Social-Democrats. Plekhanov, who after December 1905[2] faint-heartedly exclaimed: "They should not have taken up arms," had the modesty to compare himself to Marx. Marx, says he, also put the brakes on the revolution in 1870.

Yes, Marx *also* put the brakes on the revolution. But see what a gulf lies between Plekhanov and Marx, in Plekhanov's own comparison!

In November 1905, a month before the first revolutionary wave in Russia had reached its climax, Plekhanov, far from emphatically warning the proletariat, spoke directly of the necessity *to learn to use arms and to arm.* Yet, when the struggle flared up a month later, Plekhanov, without making the slightest attempt to analyse its significance, its role in the general course of events and its connection with previous forms of struggle, hastened to play the part of a penitent intellectual and exclaimed: "They should not have taken up arms."

In September 1870, six months before the Commune, Marx gave a direct warning to the French workers: insurrection would be *an act of desperate folly,* he said in the well-known Address of the International.[3] He exposed *in advance* the nationalistic illusions of the possibility of a movement in the spirit of 1792. He was able to say, *not after the event,* but many months before: "Don't take up arms."

And how did he behave when this *hopeless* cause, as he himself had called it in September, began to take practical shape in March 1871? Did he use it (as Plekhanov did the December events) to "take a dig" at his enemies, the Proudhonists and Blanquists[4] who were leading the Commune? Did he begin to scold like a schoolmistress, and say: "I told you so, I warned you; this is what comes of your romanticism, your revolutionary ravings?" Did he preach to the Communards, as Plekhanov did to the December fighters, the sermon of the smug philistine: "You should not have taken up arms?"

No. On April 12, 1871, Marx writes an *enthusiastic* letter to Kugelmann[6]—a letter which we would like to see hung in the home of every Russian Social-Democrat and of every literate Russian worker.

In September 1870 Marx had called the insurrection an act of desperate folly; but in April 1871, when he saw the mass movement of the people he watched it with the keen attention of a participant in great events marking a step forward in the historic revolutionary movement.

This is an *attempt,* he says, to smash the bureaucratic military machine, and not simply to transfer it to different hands. And he has words of the highest praise for the *"heroic"* Paris workers led by the Proudhonists and Blanquists. "What elasticity," he writes, "what historical initiative, what a capacity for sacrifice in these Parisians! . . . History has no like example of a like greatness."

The *historical initiative* of the masses was what Marx prized above everything else. Ah, if only our Russian Social-Democrats would learn from Marx how to appreciate the *historical initiative* of the Russian workers and peasants in October and December 1905!

Compare the homage paid to the *historical initiative* of the masses by a profound thinker, who foresaw failure six months ahead—and the lifeless, soulless, pedantic: "They should not have taken up arms"! Are these not as far apart as heaven and earth?

And like *a participant* in the mass struggle, to which he reacted with all his characteristic ardour and passion, Marx, then living in exile in London, set to work to criticise the *immediate steps* of the "recklessly brave" Parisians who were *"ready to storm heaven."*

Ah, how our present "realist" wiseacres among the Marxists, who in 1906-07 are deriding revolutionary romanticism in Russia, would have sneered at Marx at the time! How people would have scoffed at *a materialist, an economist,* an enemy of utopias, who pays homage to an "attempt" to storm *heaven!* What tears, condescending smiles or commiseration these "men in mufflers"[6] would have bestowed upon him for his rebel tendencies, utopianism, etc., etc., and for his appreciation of a heaven-storming movement!

But Marx was not inspired with the wisdom of the small fry who are afraid to discuss the *technique* of the higher forms of revolutionary struggle. It is precisely the *technical* problems of the insurrection that he discussed. Defence or attack, he asked, as if the military operation were taking place just outside London. And he decided that it must certainly be attack: "*They should have marched at once on Versailles.* . . ."

This was written in April 1871, a few weeks before the great and bloody May . . . .

"They should have marched at once on Versailles"—the insurgents should, those who had begun the "act of desperate folly" (September 1870) of storming heaven.

"They should not have taken up arms" in December 1905 in order to oppose by force the first attempts to take away the liberties that had been won. . . .

Yes, Plekhanov had good reason to compare himself to Marx!

"Second mistake," Marx said, continuing his *technical* criticism: "The Central Committee" (the *military command*—note this—the reference is to the Central Committee of the National Guard) "surrendered its power *too soon.* . . ."

Marx knew how to warn the *leaders* against a premature rising. But his attitude towards the heaven-storming *proletariat* was that of a practical adviser, of a participant in the *struggle* of the masses, who were raising the *whole* movement to *a higher level* in spite of the false theories and mistakes of Blanqui and Proudhon.

"However that may be," he wrote, "the present rising in Paris—even if it be crushed by the wolves, swine, and vile curs of the old society—is the most glorious deed of our Party since the June insurrection. . . ."[7]

And, without concealing from the proletariat *a single* mistake of the Commune, Marx dedicated to this *heroic deed* a work which *to this very day* serves as the best guide in the fight for "heaven" and as a frightful bugbear to the liberal and radical "*swine*."

Plekhanov dedicated to the December events a "work" which has become practically the bible of the Cadets.[8]

Yes, Plekhanov had good reason to compare himself to Marx.

Kugelmann apparently replied to Marx expressing certain doubts, referring to the hopelessness of the struggle and to realism as opposed to romanticism—at any rate, he compared the Commune, an *insurrection*, to the peaceful demonstration in Paris on June 13, 1849.

Marx immediately (April 17, 1871) severely lectured Kugelmann.[9]

"*World history*," he wrote, "*would indeed be very easy to make, if the struggle were taken up only on condition of infallibly favourable chances*."

In September 1870, Marx called the insurrection an act of desperate folly. But, when the *masses* rose, Marx wanted to march with them, to learn with them in the process of the struggle, and not to give them bureaucratic admonitions. He realised that to attempt in advance to calculate the chances *with complete accuracy* would be quackery or hopeless pedantry. What he valued *above everything else* was that the working class heroically and self-sacrificingly took the initiative in *making* world history. Marx regarded world history from the standpoint of those who *make* it without being in a position to calculate the chances *infallibly* beforehand, and not from the standpoint of an intellectual philistine who moralises: "It was easy to foresee . . . they should not have taken up. . . ."

Marx was also able to appreciate that there are moments in history when a desperate struggle of the *masses*, even for a hopeless cause, is *essential* for the further schooling of these masses and their training for the *next* struggle.

Such a *statement* of the question is quite incomprehensible and even alien in principle to our present-day quasi-Marxists, who like to take the name of Marx in vain, to borrow only his estimate of the past, and not his ability to make the future. Plekhanov did not even think of it when he set out after December 1905 *"to put the brakes on."*

But it is precisely this question that Marx raised, without in the least forgetting that he himself in September 1870 regarded insurrection as an act of desperate folly.

". . . The bourgeois *canaille* of Versailles," he wrote, ". . . presented the Parisians with the alternative of taking up the fight or succumbing without a struggle. In the latter case, the *demoralisation of the working class* would have been a *far greater* misfortune than the fall of any number of 'leaders'."[10]

And with this we shall conclude our brief review of the lessons in a policy worthy of the proletariat which Marx teaches in his letters to Kugelmann.

The working class of Russia has already proved once, and will prove again more than once, that it is capable of "storming heaven."

2. LESSONS OF THE COMMUNE[11]

AFTER THE *coup d'état,* which marked the end of the revolution of 1848, France fell under the yoke of the Napoleonic regime for a period of 18 years. This regime brought upon the country not only economic ruin but national humiliation. In rising against the old regime the proletariat undertook two tasks—one of them national and the other of a class character—the liberation of France from the German invasion and the socialist emancipation of the workers from capitalism. This union of two tasks forms a unique feature of the Commune.

The bourgeoisie had formed a "government of national defence" and the proletariat had to fight for national independence under its leadership. Actually, it was a government of "national betrayal" which saw its mission in fighting the Paris proletariat. But the proletariat, blinded by patriotic illusions, did not perceive this. The patriotic idea had its origin in the Great Revolution of the eighteenth century; it swayed the minds of the socialists of the Commune; and Blanqui, for example, undoubtedly a revolutionary and an ardent supporter of socialism, could find no better title for his newspaper than the bourgeois cry: *"The country is in danger!"*

Combining contradictory tasks—patriotism and socialism—was the fatal mistake of the French socialists. In the Manifesto of the International, issued in September 1870, Marx had warned the French proletariat against being misled by a false national idea[12]; profound changes had taken place since the Great Revolution, class antagonisms had sharpened, and whereas at that time the struggle against the whole of European reaction united the entire revolutionary nation, now the proletariat could no longer combine its interests with the interests of other classes hostile to it; let the bourgeoisie bear the responsibility for the national humiliation—the task of the proletariat was to fight for the socialist emancipation of labor from the yoke of the bourgeoisie.

And indeed the true nature of bourgeois "patriotism" was not long in revealing itself. Having concluded an ignominious peace with the Prussians, the Versailles government proceeded to its immediate task—it launched an attack to wrest the arms that terrified it from the hands of the Paris proletariat. The workers replied by proclaiming the Commune and civil war.

Although the socialist proletariat was split up into numerous sects, the Commune was a splendid example of the unanimity with which the proletariat was able to accomplish the democratic tasks which the bourgeoisie could only proclaim. Without any particularly complex legislation, in a simple, straightforward manner, the proletariat, which had seized power, carried out the democratisation of the social system, abolished the bureaucracy, and made all official posts elective.

But two mistakes destroyed the fruits of the splendid victory. The proletariat stopped half-way: instead of setting about "expropriating the expropriators," it allowed itself to be led astray by dreams of establishing a higher justice in the country united by a common national task; such institutions as the banks, for example, were not taken over, and Proudhonist theories about a "just exchange," etc., still prevailed among the socialists. The second mistake was excessive magnanimity on the part of the proletariat: instead of destroying its enemies it sought to exert moral influence on them; it underestimated the significance of direct military operations in civil war, and instead of launching a resolute offensive against Versailles that would have crowned its victory in Paris, it tarried and gave the Versailles government time to gather the dark forces and prepare for the blood-soaked week of May.

But despite all its mistakes the Commune was a superb example of the great proletarian movement of the nineteenth century. Marx set a high value on the historic significance of the Commune—if, during the treacherous attempt by the Versailles gang to seize the arms of the Paris proletariat, the workers had allowed themselves to be disarmed without a fight, the disastrous effect of the demoralisation that this weakness would have caused in the proletarian movement, would have been far, far greater than the losses suffered by the working class in the battle to defend its arms. The sacrifices of the Commune, heavy as they were, are made up for by its significance for the general struggle of the proletariat: it stirred the socialist movement throughout Europe, it demonstrated the strength of civil war, it dispelled patriotic illusions, and destroyed the naive belief in any efforts of the bourgeoisie for common national aims. The Commune taught the European proletariat to pose concretely the tasks of the socialist revolution.

The lesson learnt by the proletariat will not be forgotten. The working class will make use of it, as it has already done in Russia during the December uprising.

The period that preceded the Russian revolution and prepared it bears a certain resemblance to the period of the Napoleonic yoke in France. In Russia, too, the autocratic clique had brought upon the country economic ruin and national humiliation. But the outbreak of revolution was held back for a long time, since social development had not yet created the conditions for a mass movement and, notwithstanding all the courage displayed, the isolated actions against the government in the pre-revolutionary period broke against the apathy of the masses. Only the Social-Democrats, by strenuous and systematic work, educated the masses to the level of the higher forms of struggle—mass actions and armed civil war.

The Social-Democrats were able to shatter the "common national" and "patriotic" delusions of the young proletariat and later, when the Manifesto of October 17 [1905][13] had been wrested from the tsar due to their direct intervention, the proletariat began vigorous preparation for the next, inevitable phase of the revolution—the armed uprising. Having shed "common national" illusions, it concentrated its class forces in its own mass organisations—the Soviets of Workers' and Soldiers' Deputies, etc. And notwithstanding all the differences in the aims and tasks of the Russian revolution, compared with the French revolution of 1871, the Russian proletariat had to resort to the same method of struggle as that first used by the Paris Commune—civil war. Mindful of the lessons of the Commune, it knew that the proletariat should not ignore peaceful methods of struggle—they serve its ordinary, day-to-day interests, they are necessary in periods of preparation for revolution—but it must never forget that in certain conditions the class struggle assumes the form of armed conflict and civil war; there are times when the interests of the proletariat call for ruthless extermination of its enemies in open armed clashes. This was first demonstrated by the French proletariat in the Commune and brilliantly confirmed by the Russian proletariat in the December uprising.

And although these magnificent uprisings of the working class were crushed, there will be another uprising, in face of which the forces of the enemies of the proletariat will prove ineffective, and from which the socialist proletariat will emerge completely victorious.

3. IN MEMORY OF THE COMMUNE[14]

FORTY YEARS have passed since the proclamation of the Paris Commune. In accordance with tradition, the French workers paid homage to the memory of the men and women of the revolution of March 18, 1871, by meetings and demonstrations. At the end of May they will again place wreaths on the graves of the Communards who were shot, the victims of the terrible "May Week," and over their graves they will once more vow to fight untiringly until their ideas have triumphed and the cause they bequeathed has been fully achieved.

Why does the proletariat, not only in France but throughout the entire world, honour the men and women of the Paris Commune as their predecessors? And what is the heritage of the Commune?

The Commune sprang up spontaneously. No one consciously prepared it in an organised way. The unsuccessful war with Germany, the privations suffered during the siege, the unemployment among the proletariat and the ruin among the lower middle classes; the indignation of the masses against the upper classes and against authorities who had displayed utter incompetence, the vague unrest among the working class, which was discontented with its lot and was striving for a different social system; the reactionary composition of the National Assembly, which roused apprehensions as to the fate of the republic—all this and many other factors combined to drive the population of Paris to revolution on March 18, which unexpectedly placed power in the hands of the National Guard, in the hands of the working class and the petty bourgeoisie which had sided with it.

It was an event unprecedented in history. Up to that time power had, as a rule, been in the hands of landowners and capitalists, i.e., in the hands of their trusted agents who made up the so-called government. After the revolution of March 18, when M. Thiers' government had fled from Paris with its troops, its police and its officials, the people became masters of the situation and power passed into the hands of the proletariat. But in modern society, the proletariat, economically enslaved by capital, cannot dominate politically unless it breaks the chains which fetter it to capital. That is why the movement of the Commune was bound to take on a socialist tinge, i.e., to strive to overthrow the rule of the bourgeoisie, the rule of capital, and to destroy the very *foundations* of the contemporary social order.

At first this movement was extremely indefinite and confused. It was joined by patriots who hoped that the Commune would renew the war with the Germans and bring it to a successful conclusion. It enjoyed the support of the small shopkeepers who were threatened with ruin unless there was a postponement of payments on debts and rent (the government refused to grant this postponement, but they obtained it from the Commune). Finally, it enjoyed, at first, the sympathy of bourgeois republicans who feared that the reactionary National Assembly (the "rustics," the savage landlords) would restore the monarchy. But it was of course the workers (especially the artisans of Paris), among whom active socialist propaganda had been carried on during the last years of the Second Empire and many of whom even belonged to the International, who played the principal part in this movement.

Only the workers remained loyal to the Commune to the end. The bourgeois republicans and the petty bourgeoisie soon broke away from it: the former were frightened off by the revolutionary-socialist, proletarian character of the movement; the latter broke away when they saw that it was doomed to inevitable defeat. Only the French proletarians supported *their* government fearlessly and untiringly, they alone fought and died for it—that is to say, for the cause of the emancipation of the working class, for a better future for all toilers.

Deserted by its former allies and left without support, the Commune was doomed to defeat. The entire bourgeoisie of France, all the landlords, stockbrokers, factory owners, all the robbers, great and small, all the exploiters joined forces against it. This bourgeois coalition, supported by Bismarck (who released a hundred thousand

French prisoners of war to help crush revolutionary Paris), succeeded in rousing the ignorant peasants and the petty bourgeoisie of the provinces against the proletariat of Paris, and forming a ring of steel around half of Paris (the other half was besieged by the German army). In some of the larger cities in France (Marseilles, Lyons, St. Étienne, Dijon, etc.) the workers also attempted to seize power, to proclaim the Commune and come to the help of Paris; but these attempts were short-lived. Paris, which had first raised the banner of proletarian revolt, was left to its own resources and doomed to certain destruction.

Two conditions, at least, are necessary for a victorious social revolution—highly developed productive forces and a proletariat adequately prepared for it. But in 1871 both of these conditions were lacking. French capitalism was still poorly developed, and France at that time was mainly a petty-bourgeois country (artisans, peasants, shopkeepers, etc.). On the other hand, there was no workers' party, the working class had not gone through a long school of struggle and was unprepared, and for the most part did not even clearly visualise its tasks and the methods of fulfilling them. There was no serious political organisation of the proletariat, nor were there strong trade unions and co-operative societies. . . .

But the chief thing which the Commune lacked was time—an opportunity to take stock of the situation and to embark upon the fulfilment of its programme. It had scarcely had time to start work, when the government entrenched in Versailles and supported by the entire bourgeoisie began hostilities against Paris. The Commune had to concentrate primarily on self-defence. Right up to the very end, May 21–28, it had no time to think seriously of anything else.

However, in spite of these unfavourable conditions, in spite of its brief existence, the Commune managed to promulgate a few measures which sufficiently characterise its real significance and aims. The Commune did away with the standing army, that blind weapon in the hands of the ruling classes, and armed the whole people. It proclaimed the separation of church and state, abolished state payments to religious bodies (i.e., state salaries for priests), made popular education purely secular, and in this way struck a severe blow at the gendarmes in cassocks. In the purely social sphere the Commune accomplished very little, but this little nevertheless clearly reveals its character as a popular, workers' government. Night work in bakeries was forbidden; the system of fines, which represented legalised robbery of the workers, was abolished. Finally, there was the famous decree that all factories and workshops abandoned or shut down by their owners were to be turned over to associations of workers that were to resume production. And, as if to emphasise its character as a truly democratic, proletarian government, the Commune decreed that the salaries of all administrative and government officials, irrespective of rank, should not exceed the normal wages of a worker, and in no case amount to more than 6,000 francs a year (less than 200 rubles a month).

All these measures showed clearly enough that the Commune was a deadly menace to the old world founded on the enslavement and exploitation of the people. That was why bourgeois society could not feel at ease so long as the Red Flag of the proletariat waved over the *Hôtel de Ville* in Paris. And when the organised forces of the government finally succeeded in gaining the upper hand over the poorly organised forces of the revolution, the Bonapartist generals, who had been beaten by the Germans and who showed courage only in fighting their defeated countrymen, those French Rennenkampfs and Meller-Zakomelskys,[15] organised such a slaughter as Paris had never known. About 30,000 Parisians were shot down by the bestial soldiery, and about 45,000 were arrested, many of whom were afterwards executed, while thousands were transported or exiled. In all, Paris lost about 100,000 of its best people, including some of the finest workers in all trades.

The bourgeoisie were satisfied. "Now we have finished with socialism for a long time," said their leader, the blood-thirsty dwarf, Thiers, after he and his generals had drowned the proletariat of Paris in blood. But these bourgeois crows croaked in vain. Less than six years after the suppression of the Commune, when many of its champions were still pining in prison or in exile, a new working-class movement arose in France. A new socialist generation, enriched by the experience of their predecessors and no whit discouraged by their defeat, picked up the flag which had fallen from the hands of the fighters in the cause of the Commune and bore it boldly and confidently forward. Their battle cry was: "Long live the social revolution! Long live the Commune!" And in another few years, the new workers' party and the agitational work launched by it throughout the country compelled the ruling classes to release Communards who were still kept in prison by the government.

The memory of the fighters of the Commune is honoured not only by the workers of France but by the proletariat of the whole world. For the Commune fought, not for some local or narrow national aim, but for the emancipation of all toiling humanity, of all the downtrodden and oppressed. As a foremost fighter for the social revolution, the Commune has won sympathy wherever there is a proletariat suffering and engaged in struggle. The epic of its life and death, the sight of a workers' government which seized the capital of the world and held it for over two months, the spectacle of the heroic struggle of the proletariat and the torments it underwent after its defeat—all this raised the spirit of millions of workers, aroused their hopes and enlisted their sympathy for the cause of socialism. The thunder of the cannon in Paris awakened the most backward sections of the proletariat from their deep slumber, and everywhere gave impetus to the growth of revolutionary socialist propaganda. That is why the cause of the Commune is not dead. It lives to the present day in every one of us.

The cause of the Commune is the cause of the social revolution, the cause of the complete political and economic emancipation of the toilers. It is the cause of the proletariat of the whole world. And in this sense it is immortal.

4. EXPERIENCE OF THE PARIS COMMUNE OF 1871: MARX'S ANALYSIS[16]

A. In What Does the Heroism of the Communards Consist?

It is well known that in the autumn of 1870, a few months prior to the Commune, Marx warned the Paris workers that an attempt to overthrow the government would be the folly of despair. But when, in March 1871, a decisive battle was *forced* upon the workers and they accepted it, when the uprising had become a fact, Marx welcomed the proletarian revolution with the greatest enthusiasm, in spite of unfavourable auguries. Marx did not assume the rigid attitude of pedantically condemning an "untimely" movement as did the ill-famed Russian renegade from Marxism, Plekhanov, who, in November 1905, wrote encouragingly about the workers' and peasants' struggle but, after December 1905, cried, liberal fashion: "They should not have taken up arms."

Marx, however, was not only enthusiastic about the heroism of the Communards who "stormed the heavens," as he expressed himself. He saw in the mass revolutionary movement, although it did not attain its aim, an historic experiment of gigantic importance, a certain advance of the world proletarian revolution, a practical step more important than hundreds of programmes and discussions. To analyse this experiment, to draw from it lessons in tactics, to re-examine his theory in the new light it afforded—such was the problem as it presented itself to Marx.

The only "correction" which Marx thought it necessary to make in the *Communist Manifesto* was made by him on the basis of the revolutionary experience of the Paris Communards.

The last preface to a new German edition of the *Communist Manifesto* signed by both its authors is dated June 24, 1872. In this preface the authors, Karl Marx and Frederick Engels, say that the programme of the *Communist Manifesto* is now "in places out of date."

"One thing especially—they continue—was proved by the Commune, *viz., that the 'working class cannot simply lay hold of the ready-made state machinery and wield it for its own purposes.' "*[17]

The words within quotation marks in this passage are borrowed by its authors from Marx's book, *The Civil War in France.*

It thus appears that one principal and fundamental lesson of the Paris Commune was considered by Marx and Engels to be of such enormous importance that they introduced it as a vital correction into the *Communist Manifesto.*

It is most characteristic that it is precisely this vital correction which has been distorted by the opportunists, and its meaning, probably, is not known to nine-tenths, if not ninety-nine-hundredths, of the readers of the *Communist Manifesto.* We shall deal with this distortion more fully further on, in a chapter devoted specially to distortions.[18] It will be sufficient here to note that the current vulgar "interpretation" of Marx's famous utterance quoted above consists in asserting that Marx is here emphasising the idea of gradual development, in contradistinction to a seizure of power, and so on.

As a matter of fact, *exactly the opposite is the case.* Marx's idea is that the working class must *break up, shatter* the "ready-made state machinery," and not confine itself merely to taking possession of it.

On April 12, 1871, i.e., just at the time of the Commune, Marx wrote to Kugelmann:

"If you look at the last chapter of my *Eighteenth Brumaire* you will find that I say that the next attempt of the French Revolution will be no longer, as before, to transfer the bureaucratic-military machine from one hand to another, but to *smash* it [Marx's italics—the original is *zerbrechen*], and this is essential for every real people's revolution on the Continent. And this is what our heroic Party comrades in Paris are attempting."

In these words, "to smash the bureaucratic-military machine," is contained, briefly formulated, the principal lesson of Marxism on the tasks of the proletariat in relation to the state during a revolution. And it is just this lesson which has not only been forgotten, but downright distorted, by the prevailing Kautskyist "interpretation" of Marxism.

As for Marx's reference to the *Eighteenth Brumaire*, we have quoted above the corresponding passage in full.[19]

It is interesting to note two particular points in the passages quoted by Marx. First, he confines his conclusions to the Continent. This was natural in 1871, when England was still the model of a purely capitalist country, but without a military machine and, in large measure, without a bureaucracy. Hence Marx excluded England, where a revolution, even a people's revolution, could be imagined, and was then possible, *without* the preliminary condition of destroying the "ready-made state machinery."

Today, in 1917, in the epoch of the first great imperialist war, this exception made by Marx is no longer valid. Both England and America, the greatest and last representatives of Anglo-Saxon "liberty" in the sense of the absence of militarism and bureaucracy, have today plunged headlong into the all-European dirty, bloody morass of military bureaucratic institutions to which everything is subordinated and which trample everything under foot. Today, both in England and in America, the "precondition of any real people's revolution" is the *break-up*, the *shattering* of the "ready-made state machinery" (brought in those countries, between 1914 and 1917, to general "European" imperialist perfection).

Secondly, particular attention should be given to Marx's extremely profound remark that the destruction of the military and bureaucratic apparatus of the state is "essential for every real *people's* revolution." This idea of a "people's" revolution seems strange on Marx's lips, and the Russian Plekhanovists and Mensheviks, those followers of Struve[20] who wish to be considered Marxists, might possibly declare such an expression to be a "slip of the tongue." They have reduced Marxism to such a state of poverty-stricken "liberal" distortion that nothing exists for them beyond the distinction between bourgeois and proletarian revolution—and even that distinction they understand in an entirely lifeless way.

If we take for examples the revolutions of the twentieth century, we shall, of course, have to recognise both the Portuguese and the Turkish revolutions as bourgeois. Neither, however, is a "people's" revolution, inasmuch as the mass of the people, the enormous majority, does not make its appearance actively, independently, with its own economic and political demands, in either the one or the other. On the other hand, the Russian bourgeois revolution of 1905-1907, although it presented no such "brilliant" successes as at times fell to the lot of the Portuguese and Turkish revolutions, was undoubtedly a real "people's" revolution, since the mass of the people, the majority, the lowest social "depths," crushed down by oppression and exploitation, were rising independently, since they put on the entire course of the revolution the stamp of *their* demands, *their* attempts at building up, in their own way, a new society in place of the old society that was being shattered.

In the Europe of 1871, the proletariat on the Continent did not constitute the majority of the people. A "people's" revolution, actually sweeping the majority into its current, could be such only if it embraced both the proletariat and the peasantry. Both classes then constituted the "people." Both classes are united by the circumstance that the "bureaucratic and military state machinery" oppresses, crushes, exploits them. To *shatter* this machinery, to *break it up*—this is the true interest of the "people," of its majority, the workers and most of the peasants, this is the "preliminary condition" of a free union of the poorest peasantry with the proletarians; while, without such a union, democracy is unstable and Socialist reorganisation is impossible.

Towards such a union, as is well known, the Paris Commune was making its way, though it did not reach its goal, owing to a number of circumstances, internal and external.

Consequently, when speaking of "a real people's revolution," Marx, without in the least forgetting the peculiar characteristics of the petty bourgeoisie (he spoke of them much and often), was very carefully taking into account the actual interrelation of classes in most of the continental European states in 1871. On the other hand, he stated that the "breaking up" of the state machinery is demanded by the interests both of the workers and of the peasants, that it unites them, that it places before them the common task of removing the "parasite" and replacing it by something new.

B. What Is to Replace the Shattered State Machinery?

In 1847, in the *Communist Manifesto*, Marx answered this question still in a purely abstract manner, stating the problems rather than the methods of solving them. To replace this machinery by "the proletariat organised as the ruling class," by "establishing democracy"—such was the answer of the *Communist Manifesto*.

Without resorting to Utopias, Marx waited for the *experience* of a mass movement to produce the answer to the problem as to the exact forms which this organisation of the proletariat as the ruling class will assume and as to the exact manner in which this organisation will be combined with the most complete, most consistent "establishment of democracy."

The experiment of the Commune, meagre as it was, was subjected by Marx to the most careful analysis in his *The Civil War in France*. Let us quote the most important passages of this work.

There developed in the nineteenth century, he says, originating from the days of absolute monarchy, "the centralised state power, with its ubiquitous organs of standing army, police, bureaucracy, clergy and judicature." With the development of class antagonism between capital and labour, "the state power assumed more and more the character of the national power of capital over labour, of a public force organised for social enslavement, of an engine of class despotism. After every revolution marking a progressive phase in the class struggle, the purely repressive character of the state power stands out in bolder and bolder relief." The state power, after the revolution of 1848–1849 became "the national war engine of capital against labour." The Second Empire consolidated this.

"The direct antithesis of the Empire was the Commune," says Marx. It was the "positive form" of "a republic that was not only to supersede the monarchical form of class rule, but class rule itself."

What was this "positive" form of the proletarian, the Socialist republic? What was the state it was beginning to create?

"The first decree of the Commune . . . was the suppression of the standing army, and the substitution for it of the armed people," says Marx.[21]

This demand now figures in the programme of every party calling itself Socialist. But the value of their programmes is best shown by the behaviour of our Socialist-Revolutionaries and Mensheviks, who, even after the revolution of March 12, 1917, refused to carry out this demand in practice!

"The Commune was formed of municipal councilors, chosen by universal suffrage in various wards of the town, responsible and revocable at short terms. The majority of its members were naturally working men, or acknowledged representatives of the working class. . . . Instead of continuing to be the agent of the Central Government, the police was at once stripped of its political attributes, and turned into the responsible and at all times revocable agent of the Commune. So were the officials of all other branches of the administration. From the members of the Commune downwards, the public service had to be done at *workmen's wages*. The vested interests and the representation allowances of the high dignitaries of state disappeared along with the high dignitaries themselves. . . .

"Having once got rid of the standing army and the police, the physical force elements of the old government, the Commune was anxious to break the spiritual force of repression, the "parson power." . . .

"The judicial functionaries were to be divested of [their] sham independence. . . . Like the rest of public servants, magistrates and judges were to be elective, responsible and revocable."[22]

Thus the Commune would appear to have replaced the shattered state machinery "only" by fuller democracy: abolition of the standing army; all officials to be fully elective and subjective to recall. But, as a matter of fact this "only" signifies a gigantic replacement of one type of institution by others of a fundamentally different order. Here we observe a case of "transformation of quantity into quality": democracy, introduced as fully and consistently as is gen-

erally thinkable, is transformed from capitalist democracy into proletarian democracy; from the state (i.e., a special force for the
suppression of a particular class) into something which is no longer
really the state in the accepted sense of the word.

It is still necessary to suppress the bourgeoisie and crush its resistance. This was particularly necessary for the Commune; and one of
the reasons of its defeat was that it did not do this with sufficient determination. But the organ of suppression is now the majority of the
population, and not a minority, as was always the case under slavery,
serfdom, and wage labour. And, once the majority of the people
itself suppresses its oppressors, a "special force" for suppression is
no longer necessary. In this sense the state *begins to wither away*.
Instead of the special institutions of a privileged minority (privileged
officialdom, heads of a standing army), the majority can itself
directly fulfill all these functions; and the more the discharge of the
functions of state power devolves upon the people generally, the less
need is there for the existence of this power.

In this connection the Commune's measure emphasised by Marx,
particularly worthy of note, is: the abolition of all representation
allowances, and of all money privileges in the case of officials, the
reduction of the remuneration of *all* servants of the state to "*workingmen's wages*." Here is shown, more clearly than anywhere else,
the *break* from a bourgeois democracy to a proletarian democracy,
from the democracy of the oppressors to the democracy of the oppressed classes, from the state as a "special force for suppression" of
a given class to the suppression of the oppressors by the *whole force*
of the majority of the people—the workers and the peasants. And
it is precisely on this most striking point, perhaps the most important as far as the problem of the state is concerned, that the
teachings of Marx have been entirely forgotten! In popular com-
mentaries, whose number is legion, this is not mentioned. It is
"proper" to keep silent about it as if it were a piece of old-fashioned
"naïveté," just as the Christians, after Christianity had attained
the position of a state religion, "forgot" the "naïvetés" of primitive
Christianity with its democratic-revolutionary spirit.

The reduction of the remuneration of the highest state officials seems "simply" a demand of naïve, primitive democracy. One of the "founders" of modern opportunism, the former Social-Democrat, Eduard Bernstein,[23] has more than once exercised his talents in repeating the vulgar bourgeois jeers at "primitive" democracy. Like all opportunists, including the present Kautskyists,[24] he fails completely to understand that, first of all, the transition from capitalism to socialism is *impossible* without "return," in a measure, to "primitive" democracy (how can one otherwise pass on to the discharge of all the state functions by the majority of the population and by every individual of the population?); and, secondly, he forgets that "primitive democracy" on the basis of capitalism and capitalist culture is not the same primitive democracy as in prehistoric or precapitalist times. Capitalist culture has *created* large-scale production, factories, railways, the postal service, telephones, etc., and *on this basis* the great majority of functions of the old "state power" have become so simplified and can be reduced to such simple operations of registration, filing and checking that they will be quite within the reach of every literate person, and it will be possible to perform them for "workingmen's wages," which circumstance can (and must) strip those functions of every shadow of privilege, of every appearance of "official grandeur."

All officials, without exception, elected and subject to recall *at any time,* their salaries reduced to "workingmen's wages"—these simple and "self-evident" democratic measures, which, completely uniting the interests of the workers and the majority of peasants, at the same time serve as a bridge leading from capitalism to Socialism. These measures refer to the state, to the purely political reconstruction of society; but, of course, they acquire their full meaning and significance only in connection with the "expropriation of the expropriators," either accomplished or in preparation, *i.e.,* with the turning of capitalist private ownership of the means of production into social ownership. Marx wrote:

"The Commune made that catchword of bourgeois revolutions, cheap government, a reality by destroying the two greatest sources of expenditure—the standing army and state functionarism."[25]

From the peasantry, as from other sections of the petty bourgeoisie, only an insignificant few "rise to the top," occupy "a place in the sun" in the bourgeois sense, *i.e.*, become either well-to-do people or secure and privileged officials. The great majority of peasants in every capitalist country where the peasantry exists (and the majority of capitalist countries are of this kind) is oppressed by the government and longs for its overthrow, longs for "cheap" government. This can be realised *only* by the proletariat; and by realising it, the proletariat makes at the same time a step towards the Socialist reconstruction of the state.

C. THE DESTRUCTION OF PARLIAMENTARISM

"The Commune—says Marx—was to be a working, not a parliamentary body, executive and legislative at the same time. . . .

"Instead of deciding once in three or six years which member of the ruling class was to represent the people in Parliament, universal suffrage was to serve the people, constituted in Communes, as individual suffrage serves every other employer in the search for the workmen and managers in his business."[26]

This remarkable criticism of parliamentarism made in 1871 also belongs to the "forgotten words" of Marxism, thanks to the prevalence of social-chauvinism and opportunism. Ministers and professional parliamentarians, traitors to the proletariat and Socialist "sharks" of our day, have left all criticism of parliamentarism to the Anarchists, and, on this wonderfully intelligent ground, denounce *all* criticism of parliamentarism as "Anarchism"!! It is not surprising that the proletariat of the most "advanced" parliamentary countries, being disgusted with such "Socialists" as Messrs. Scheidemann, David, Legien, Sembat, Renaudel, Henderson, Vandervelde, Stauning, Branting, Bissolati and Co., has been giving its sympathies more and more to Anarcho-syndicalism, in spite of the fact that it is but the twin brother of opportunism.

But to Marx, revolutionary dialectics was never the empty fashionable phrase, the toy rattle, which Plekhanov, Kautsky and the others have made of it. Marx knew how to break with Anarchism ruthlessly for its inability to make use of the "stable" of bourgeois parliamentarism, especially at a time when the situation was not revolutionary; but at the same time he knew how to subject parliamentarism to a really revolutionary-proletarian criticism.

To decide once every few years which member of the ruling class is to repress and oppress the people through parliament—this is the real essence of bourgeois parliamentarism, not only in parliamentary-constitutional monarchies, but also in the most democratic republics.

But, if the question of the state is raised, if parliamentarism is to be regarded as one institution of the state, what then, from the point of view of the tasks of the proletariat in *this* realm, is to be the way out of parliamentarism? How can we do without it?

Again and again we must repeat: the teaching of Marx, based on the study of the Commune, has been so completely forgotten that any criticism of parliamentarism other than Anarchist or reactionary is quite unintelligible to a present-day "Social-Democrat" (read: present-day traitor to Socialism).

The way out of parliamentarism is to be found, of course, not in the abolition of the representative institutions and the elective principle, but in the conversion of the representative institutions from mere "talking shops" into working bodies. "The Commune was to be a working, not a parliamentary body, executive and legislative at the same time."

"A working, not a parliamentary body"—this hits the vital spot of present-day parliamentarians and the parliamentary Social-Democratic "lap-dogs"! Take any parliamentary country, from America to Switzerland, from France to England, Norway and so forth—the actual work of the "state" there is done behind the scenes and is carried out by the departments, the offices and the staffs. Parliament itself is given up to talk for the special purpose of fooling the "common people." This is so true that even in the Russian republic,[27] a bourgeois-democratic republic, all these aims of parliamentarism were immediately revealed, even before a real parliament was created. Such heroes of rotten philistinism as the Skobelevs and the Tseretelis, Chernovs and Avksentyevs, have managed to pollute even the Soviets, after the model of the most despicable petty-bourgeois parliamentarism, by turning them into hollow talking shops. In the Soviets, the Right Honourable "Socialist" Ministers are fooling the confiding peasants with phrase-mongering and resolutions. In the government itself a sort of permanent quadrille is going on in order that, on the one hand, as many S.-R.'s and Mensheviks as possible may get at the "gravy," the "soft" jobs, and, on the other hand, the attention of the people may be occupied. All the while the real "state" business is being done in the offices, in the staffs.

The *Dyelo Naroda,* organ of the ruling Socialist-Revolutionary Party, recently admitted in an editorial article—with the incomparable candour of people of "good society," in which "all" are engaged in political prostitution—that even in those ministries which belong to the "Socialists" (please excuse the term), the whole bureaucratic apparatus remains essentially the same as of old, working as of old, and "freely" obstructing revolutionary measures. Even if we did not have this admission, would not the actual history of the participation of the S.-R.'s and Mensheviks in the government prove this? It is only characteristic that—while in ministerial company with the Cadets—Messrs. Chernov, Rusanov, Zenzinov and other editors of the *Dyelo Naroda* have so completely lost all shame that they unblushingly proclaim, as if it were a mere bagatelle, that in "their" ministries everything remains as of old!! Revolutionary-democratic phrases to gull the Simple Simons; bureaucracy and red tape for the "benefit" of the capitalists—here you have the *essence* of the "honourable" coalition.

The venal and rotten parliamentarism of bourgeois society is replaced in the Commune by institutions in which freedom of opinion and discussion does not degenerate into deception, for the parliamentarians must themselves work, must themselves execute their own laws, must themselves verify their results in actual life, must themselves be directly responsible to their electorate. Representative institutions remain, but parliamentarism as a special system, as a division of labour between the legislative and the executive functions, as a privileged position for the deputies, *no longer exists.* Without representative institutions we cannot imagine democracy, not even proletarian democracy; but we can and *must* think of democracy without parliamentarism, if criticism of bourgeois society is not mere empty words for us, if the desire to overthrow the rule of the bourgeoisie is our serious and sincere desire, and not a mere "election cry" for catching workingmen's votes, as it is with the Mensheviks and S.-R.'s, the Scheidemanns, the Legiens, the Sembats and the Vanderveldes.

It is most instructive to notice that, in speaking of the functions of *those* officials who are necessary both in the Commune and in the proletarian democracy, Marx compares them with the workers of "every other employer," that is, of the usual capitalist concern, with its "workers and managers."

There is no trace of Utopianism in Marx, in the sense of inventing or imagining a "new" society. No, he studies, as a process of natural history, the *birth* of the new society *from* the old, the forms of transition from the latter to the former. He takes the actual experience of a mass proletarian movement and tries to draw practical lessons from it. He "learns" from the Commune, as all great revolutionary thinkers have not been afraid to learn from the experience of great movements of the oppressed classes, never preaching them pedantic "sermons" (such as Plekhanov's: "They should not have taken up arms"; or Tsereteli's: "A class must know how to limit itself").

To destroy officialdom immediately, everywhere, completely— this cannot be thought of. That is a Utopia. But to *break up* at once the old bureaucratic machine and to start immediately the construction of a new one which will enable us gradually to reduce all officialdom to naught—this is *no* Utopia, it is the experience of the Commune, it is the direct and urgent task of the revolutionary proletariat.

Capitalism simplifies the functions of "state" administration; it makes it possible to throw off "commanding" methods and to reduce everything to a matter of the organisation of the proletarians (as the ruling class), hiring "workmen and managers" in the name of the whole of society.

We are not Utopians, we do not indulge in "dreams" of how best to do away *immediately* with all administration, with all subordination; these Anarchist dreams, based upon a lack of understanding of the task of proletarian dictatorship, are basically foreign to Marxism, and, as a matter of fact, they serve but to put off the Socialist revolution until human nature is different. No, we want the Socialist revolution with human nature as it is now, with human nature that cannot do without subordination, control, and "managers."

But if there be subordination, it must be to the armed vanguard of all the exploited and the labouring—to the proletariat. The specific "commanding" methods of the state officials can and must begin to be replaced—immediately, within twenty-four hours—by the simple functions of "managers" and bookkeepers, functions which are now already within the capacity of the average city dweller and can well be performed for "workingmen's wages."

We organise large-scale production, starting from what capitalism has already created; we workers *ourselves,* relying on our own experience as workers, establishing a strict, an iron discipline, supported by the state power of the armed workers, shall reduce the role of the state officials to that of simply carrying out our instructions as responsible, moderately paid "managers" (of course, with technical knowledge of all sorts, types and degrees). This is *our* proletarian task, with this we can and *must begin* when carrying through a proletarian revolution. Such a beginning, on the basis of large-scale production, of itself leads to the gradual "withering away" of all bureaucracy, to the gradual creation of a new order, an order without quotation marks, an order which has nothing to do with wage slavery, an order in which the more and more simplified functions of control and accounting will be performed by each in turn, will then become a habit, and will finally die out as *special* functions of a special stratum of the population.

A witty German Social-Democrat of the 'seventies of the last century called the *post office* an example of the socialist system. This is very true. At present the post office is a business organised on the lines of a state *capitalist* monopoly. Imperialism is gradually transforming all trusts into organisations of a similar type. Above the "common" workers, who are overloaded with work and starving, there stands here the same bourgeois bureaucracy. But the mechanism of social management is here already to hand. Overthrow the capitalists, crush with the iron hand of the armed workers the resistance of these exploiters, break the bureaucratic machine of the modern state—and you have before you a mechanism of the highest technical equipment, freed of "parasites," capable of being set into motion by the united workers themselves who hire their own technicians, managers, bookkeepers, and pay them *all*, as, indeed, every "state" official, with the usual workers' wage. Here is a concrete, practicable task, immediately realisable in relation to all trusts, a task that frees the workers of exploitation and makes use of the experience (especially in the realm of the construction of the state) which the Commune began to reveal in practice.

To organise the *whole* national economy like the postal system, in such a way that the technicians, managers, bookkeepers as well as *all* officials, should receive no higher wages than "workingmen's wages," all under the control and leadership of the armed proletariat—this is our immediate aim. This is the kind of state and economic basis we need. This is what will produce the destruction of parliamentarism, while retaining representative institutions. This is what will free the labouring classes from the prostitution of these institutions by the bourgeoisie.

D. The Organisation of National Unity

"In a rough sketch of national organisation which the Commune had no time to develop, it states clearly that the Commune was to be the political form of even the smallest country hamlet. . . ."

From these Communes would be elected the "National Delegation" at Paris.

"The few but important functions which still would remain for a central government were not to be suppressed, as has been intentionally misstated, but were to be discharged by Communal, and therefore strictly responsible agents. The unity of the nation was not to be broken, but, on the contrary, to be organised by the Communal constitution, and to become a reality by the destruction of the state power which claimed to be the embodiment of that unity independent of, and superior to, the nation itself, from which it was but a parisitic excrescence. While the merely repressive organs of the old governmental power were to be amputated, its legitimate functions were to be wrested from an authority usurping pre-eminence over society itself, and restored to the responsible agents of society."[28]

To what extent the opportunists of contemporary Social-Democracy have failed to understand—or perhaps it would be more true to say, did not want to understand—these observations of Marx, is best shown by the famous (Herostrates-fashion) book of the renegade Berstein, *Die Voraussetzungen des Sozialismus und die Aufgaben der Sozialdemokratie.*[29] It is just in connection with the above passage from Marx that Bernstein wrote saying that this programme

". . . in its political content displays, in all its essential features, the greatest similarity to the federalism of Proudhon. . . . In spite of all the other points of difference between Marx and the 'petty-bourgeois' Proudhon [Bernstein places the words 'petty-bourgeois' in quotation marks in order to make them sound ironical] on these points their ways of thinking resemble each other as closely as could be.

Of course, Bernstein continues, the importance of the municipalities is growing but:

". . . it seems to me doubtful whether the first task of democracy would be such a dissolution [*Auflösung*] of the modern states and such a complete transformation [*Umwandlung*] of their organisation as is described by Marx and Proudhon (the formation of a national assembly from delegates of the provincial or district assemblies, which, in their turn, would consist of delegates from the Communes), so that the whole previous mode of national representation would vanish completely."

This is really monstrous: thus to confuse Marx's views on the "destruction of the state power," of the "parasitic excrescence" with the federalism of Proudhon! But this is no accident, for it never occurs to the opportunist that Marx is not speaking here at all of federalism as opposed to centralism, but of the destruction of the old bourgeois state machinery which exists in all bourgeois countries.

To the opportunist occurs only what he sees around him, in a society of petty-bourgeois philistinism and "reformist" stagnation, namely, only "municipalities"! As for a proletarian revolution, the opportunist has forgotten even how to imagine it.

It is amusing. But it is remarkable that on this point nobody argued against Bernstein! Bernstein has been refuted often enough, especially by Plekhanov in Russian literature and by Kautsky in European, but neither made *any* remark upon *this* perversion of Marx by Bernstein.

To such an extent has the opportunist forgotten to think in a revolutionary way and forgotten how to reflect on revolution, that he attributes "federalism" to Marx, mixing him up with the founder of Anarchism, Proudhon. And Kautsky and Plekhanov, anxious to be orthodox Marxists and to defend the teaching of revolutionary Marxism, are silent on this point! Herein lies one of the roots of that vulgarisation of the ideas concerning the difference between Marxism and Anarchism, which is common to both Kautskyists and opportunists, and which we shall discuss later.

Federalism is not touched upon in Marx's observation about the experience of the Commune, as quoted above. Marx agrees with Proudhon precisely on that point which has quite escaped the opportunist Bernstein. Marx differs from Proudhon just on the point where Bernstein sees their agreement.

Marx agrees with Proudhon in that they both stand for the "destruction" of the contemporary state machinery. This common ground of Marxism with Anarchism (both with Proudhon and with Bakunin[30]) neither the opportunists nor the Kautskyists wish to see, for on this point they have themselves departed from Marxism.

Marx differs both from Proudhon and Bakunin precisely on the point of federalism (not to speak of the dictatorship of the proletariat). Federalism arises, as a principle, from the petty-bourgeois views of Anarchism. Marx is a centralist. In the above-quoted observations of his there is no deviation from centralism. Only people full of petty-bourgeois "superstitious faith" in the state can mistake the destruction of the bourgeois state for the destruction of central-ism.

But will it not be centralism if the proletariat and poorest peas-antry take the power of the state in their own hands, organise themselves freely into communes, and *unite* the action of all the com-munes in striking at capital, in crushing the resistance of the capi-talists, in the transfer of private property in railways, factories, land, and so forth, to the *entire* nation, to the whole of society? Will that not be the most consistent democratic centralism? And proletarian centralism at that?

Bernstein simply cannot conceive the possibility of voluntary cen-tralism, of a voluntary union of the communes into a nation, a voluntary fusion of the proletarian communes in the process of de-stroying bourgeois supremacy and the bourgeois state machinery. Like all philistines, Bernstein can imagine centralism only as some-thing from above, to be imposed and maintained solely by means of bureaucracy and militarism.

Marx, as though he foresaw the possibility of the perversion of his ideas, purposely emphasises that the accusation against the Com-mune that it desired to destroy the unity of the nation, to do away with a central power, was a deliberate falsehood. Marx purposely uses the phrase "to organise the unity of the nation," so as to con-trast conscious, democratic, proletarian centralism to bourgeois, military, bureaucratic centralism.

But no one is so deaf as he who will not hear. The opportunists of contemporary Social-Democracy do not, on any account, want to hear of destroying the state power, of cutting off the parasite.

E. DESTRUCTION OF THE PARASITE-STATE

We have already quoted part of Marx's statements on this subject, and must now complete his presentation.

"It is generally the fate of completely new historical creations—wrote Marx—to be mistaken for the counterpart of older and even defunct forms of social life, to which they may bear a certain likeness. Thus, this new Commune, which breaks [*bricht*] the modern state power, has been mistaken for a reproduction of the mediæval Communes . . . for a federation of small states [Montesquieu, the Girondins] . . . for an exaggerated form of the ancient struggle against over-centralisation. . . . The Communal Constitution would have restored to the social body all the forces hitherto absorbed by the state parasite feeding upon, and clogging the free movements of, society. By this one act it would have initiated the regeneration of France . . . the Communal Constitution brought the rural producers under the intellectual lead of the central towns of their districts, and there secured to them, in the working man, the natural trustees of their interests. The very existence of the Commune involved, as a matter of course, local municipal liberty, but no longer as a check upon the now superseded state power."[31]

"Breaks the modern state power," which was a "parasitic excrescence"; its "amputation," its "destruction"; "the now superseded state power"—these are the expressions used by Marx regarding the state when he appraised and analysed the experience of the Commune.

All this was written a little less than half a century ago; and now one has to undertake excavations, as it were, in order to bring uncorrupted Marxism to the knowledge of the masses. The conclusions drawn from the observation of the last great revolution, through which Marx lived, have been forgotten just at the moment when the time had arrived for the next great proletarian revolutions.

"The multiplicity of interpretations to which the Commune has been subjected, and the multiplicity of interests which construed it in their favour, show that it was a thoroughly expansive political form, while all previous forms of government had been emphatically repressive. Its true secret was this. It was essentially *a working-class government*, the product of the struggle of the producing against the appropriating class, the political form at last discovered under which to work out the economical emancipation of labour.

"Except on this last condition, the Communal Constitution would have been an impossibility and a delusion."[32] [Lenin's italics.]

The Utopians busied themselves with the "discovery" of the political forms under which the Socialist reconstruction of society could take place. The Anarchists turned away from the question of political forms altogether. The opportunists of modern Social-Democracy accepted the bourgeois political forms of a parliamentary, democratic state as the limit which cannot be overstepped; they broke their foreheads praying before this idol, denouncing as Anarchism every attempt to *destroy* these forms.

Marx deducted from the whole history of Socialism and political struggle that the state was bound to disappear, and that the transitional form of its disappearance (the transition from the political state to no state) would be the "proletariat organised as the ruling class." But Marx did not undertake the task of *discovering* the political *forms* of this future stage. He limited himself to an exact observation of French history, its analysis and the conclusion to which the year 1851 had led, *viz.,* that matters were moving towards the *destruction* of the bourgeois machinery of state.

And when the mass revolutionary movement of the proletariat burst forth, Marx, in spite of the failure of that movement, in spite of its short life and its patent weakness, began to study what political forms it had *disclosed*.

The Commune is the form "at last discovered" by the proletarian revolution, under which the economic liberation of labour can proceed.

The Commune is the first attempt of a proletarian revolution to *break up* the bourgeois state machinery and constitutes the political form, "at last discovered," which can and must *take the place* of the broken machine.

We shall see below that the Russian Revolutions of 1905 and 1917, in different surroundings and under different circumstances, continued the work of the Commune and confirmed the historic analysis made by the genius of Marx.

5. THE COMMUNE AND THE SOVIETS[33]

OUR TASK is to define the Soviet type of state. I have tried to outline theoretical views on this question in my book *State and Revolution*. It seems to me that the Marxist view on the state has been distorted in the highest degree by the official socialism that is dominant in Western Europe, and that this has been splendidly confirmed by the experience of the Soviet revolution and the establishment of the Soviets in Russia. There is much that is crude and unfinished in our Soviets; there is no doubt about that, it is obvious to everyone who examines their work; but what is important, has historical value and is a step forward in the world development of socialism, is that they are a new type of state. The Paris Commune was a matter of a few weeks, in one city, without the people being conscious of what they were doing. The Commune was not understood by those who created it; they estabilshed the Commune by following the unfailing instinct of the awakened people, and neither of the groups of French socialists was conscious of what it was doing. Because we are standing on the shoulders of the Paris Commune and the many years of development of German Social-Democracy, we have conditions that enable us to see clearly what we are doing in creating Soviet power. Despite all the crudity and lack of discipline that exist in the Soviets—this is a survival of the petty-bourgeois nature of our country—despite all that, the new type of state has been created by the masses of the people. It has been functioning for months and not weeks, and not in one city, but throughout a tremendous country, populated by several nations. This type of Soviet power has shown its value. . . .

Soviet power is machinery, machinery that will enable the masses to begin right away learning to govern the state and organise production on a nation-wide scale. It is a task of tremendous difficulty. It is, however, historically important that we are setting about its fulfilment, and not only from the point of view of our one country;

we are calling upon European workers to help. We must give a concrete explanation of our Programme from precisely that common point of view. That is why we consider it a continuation of the road taken by the Paris Commune. That is why we are confident that the European workers will be able to help once they have entered on that path. . . .

We say that if ever we are thrown back, while not rejecting the use of bourgeois parliamentarism—if hostile class forces drive us to that old position—we shall aim at what has been gained by experience, at Soviet power, at the Soviet type of state, at the Paris Commune type of state. That must be expressed in the Programme. . . .

6. BOURGEOIS DEMOCRACY[34]

THE PARIS Commune—to which all who parade as socialists pay lip service, for they know that the workers ardently and sincerely sympathise with the Commune—showed very clearly the historically conventional nature and limited value of the bourgeois parliamentary system and bourgeois democracy—institutions which, though highly progressive compared with medieval times, inevitably require a radical alteration in the era of proletarian revolution. It was Marx who best appraised the historical significance of the Commune. In his analysis, he revealed the exploiting nature of bourgeois democracy and the bourgeois parliamentary system under which the oppressed classes enjoy the right to decide once in several years which representative of the propertied classes shall "represent and suppress" (*ver- und zertreten*) the people in parliament. And it is now, when the Soviet movement is embracing the entire world and continuing the work of the Commune for all to see, that the traitors to socialism are forgetting the concrete experience and concrete lessons of the Paris Commune and repeating the old bourgeois rubbish about "democracy in general." The Commune was not a parliamentary institution.

The significance of the Commune, furthermore, lies in the fact that it endeavoured to crush, to smash to its very foundations, the bourgeois state apparatus, the bureaucratic, judicial, military and police machine, and to replace it by a self-governing, mass workers' organization in which there was no division between legislative and executive power. All contemporary bourgeois-democratic republics, including the German republic, which the traitors to socialism, in mockery of the truth, describe as a proletarian republic, retain this state apparatus. We therefore again get quite clear confirmation of the point that shouting in defence of "democracy in general" is actually defence of the bourgeoisie and their privileges as exploiters. . . .

7. A NEW TYPE OF STATE EMERGING FROM OUR REVOLUTION[35]

THE SOVIETS of Workers', Soldiers', Peasants' and other Deputies are not understood, not only in the sense that their class significance, their role in the *Russian* revolution, is not clear to the majority. They are not understood also in the sense that they constitute a new form or, rather, a new *type of state*.

The most perfect, the most advanced type of bourgeois state is the *parliamentary democratic republic:* power is vested in parliament; the state machine, the apparatus and organs of administration, is of the customary kind: the standing army, the police, and the bureaucracy—which in practice is undisplaceable, is privileged and stands *above* the people.

Since the end of the nineteenth century, however, revolutionary epochs have advanced a *higher* type of democratic state, a state which in certain respects, as Engels put it, ceases to be a state, is "no longer a state in the proper sense of the word."[36] This is a state of the Paris Commune type, one in which a standing army and police divorced from the people are *replaced* by the direct arming of the people themselves. It is *this feature* that constitutes the very essence of the Commune, which has been so misrepresented and slandered by the bourgeois writers, and to which has been erroneously ascribed, among other things, the intention of immediately "introducing" socialism.

This is the type of state which the Russian revolution *began* to create in 1905 and in 1917. A Republic of Soviets of Workers', Soldiers', Peasants', and other Deputies, united in an All-Russian Constituent Assembly of people's representatives or in a Council of Soviets, etc., is what is *already being realised* in our country now, at this juncture. It is being realised by the initiative of the nation's millions, who are creating a democracy on their own, *in their own way,* without waiting until the Cadet professors draft their legislative bills for a parliamentary bourgeois republic, or until the pedants and routine-worshippers of petty-bourgeois "Social-Democracy," like Mr. Plekhanov or Kautsky, stop distorting the Marxist teaching on the state.

Marxism differs from Anarchism in that it recognises the *need* for a state and for state power in the period of revolution in general, and in the period of transition from capitalism to socialism in particular.

Marxism differs from the petty-bourgeois, opportunist "Social-Democratism" of Plekhanov, Kautsky and Co. in that it recognises that what is required during these two periods is *not* a state of the usual parliamentary bourgeois republican type, but a state of the Paris Commune type.

The main distinctions between a state of the latter type and the old state are as follows.

It is quite easy (as history proves) to revert from a parliamentary bourgeois republic to a monarchy, for all the machinery of oppression—the army, the police, and the bureaucracy—is left intact. The Commune and the Soviets *smash* that machinery and do away with it.

The parliamentary bourgeois republic hampers and stifles the independent political life of the *masses,* their direct participation in the *democratic* organisation of the life of the state from the bottom up. The opposite is the case with the Soviets.

The latter reproduce the type of state which was being evolved by the Paris Commune and which Marx described as "the political form at last discovered under which to work out the economic emancipation of labour.[87]

We are usually told that the Russian people are not yet prepared for the "introduction" of the Commune. This was the argument of the serf-owners when they claimed that the peasants were not prepared for emancipation. The Commune, i.e., the Soviets, does not "introduce," does not intend to "introduce," and must not introduce *any* reforms which have not absolutely matured both in economic reality and in the minds of the overwhelming majority of the people. The deeper the economic collapse and the crisis produced by the war, the more urgent becomes the need for the most perfect political form, which will *facilitate* the healing of the terrible wounds inflicted on mankind by the war. The less the organisational experience of the Russian people, the more resolutely must we *proceed* to organisational development by the *people themselves,* and not merely by the bourgeois politicians and "well-placed" bureaucrats.

cream] of the Paris *canaille*." After Vinoy's rout, he must needs appear upon the scene of action in the quality of an amateur spy. The Central Committee and the Paris working men were as much responsible for the killing of Clement Thomas and Lecomte as the Princess of Wales for the fate of the people crushed to death on the day of her entrance into London.

The massacre of unarmed citizens in the Place Vendôme is a myth which M. Thiers and the Rurals persistently ignored in the Assembly, entrusting its propagation exclusively to the servants' hall of European journalism. "The men of order," the reactionists of Paris, trembled at the victory of the 18th of March. To them it was the signal of popular retribution at last arriving. The ghosts of the victims assassinated at their hands from the days of June 1848, down to the 22nd of January, 1871,[44] arose before their faces. Their panic was their only punishment. Even the *sergents-de-ville*, instead of being disarmed and locked up, as ought to have been done, had the gates of Paris flung wide open for their safe retreat to Versailles. The men of order were left not only unharmed, but allowed to rally and quietly to seize more than one stronghold in the very centre of Paris. This indulgence of the Central Committee —this magnanimity of the armed working men—so strangely at variance with the habits of the "Party of Order," the latter misinterpreted as mere symptoms of conscious weakness. Hence their silly plan to try, under the cloak of an unarmed demonstration, what Vinoy had failed to perform with his cannon and *mitrailleuses*. On the 22nd of March a riotous mob of swells started from the quarters of luxury, all the *petits crevés* in their ranks, and at their head the notorious familiars of the empire—the Heeckeren, Coëtlogon, Henri de Pène, etc. Under the cowardly pretence of a pacific demonstration, this rabble, secretly armed with the weapons of the bravo, fell into marching order, ill treated and disarmed the detached patrols and sentries of the National Guard they met with on their progress, and, on debouching from the Rue de la Paix, with the cry of "Down with the Central Committee! Down with the assassins! The National Assembly for ever!" attempted to break through the line drawn up there, and thus to carry by surprise

NOTES FOR PART ONE

1. The wars (1813-14) of the German states, led by Prussia in alliance with tsardom, against Napoleon I who annexed part of German territory to France and made the remainder subordinate to him.

2. A quotation from the second Address of the General Council on the Franco-Prussian War. Marx foresaw that after the annexation of Alsace-Lorraine, France would be thirsting for revenge and would seek allies, turning in the first place to tsarist Russia. On September 1, 1870, Marx wrote to Sorge:

"What the Prussian jackasses do not see is that the present war is leading just as inevitably to a war between Germany and Russia as the war of 1866 led to the war between Prussia and France. That is the *best result* I expect from Germany. 'Prussianism' as such never has existed, and never can exist, except in alliance with and in subjection to Russia. And such a war No. 2 will act as the midwife to the inevitable social revolution in Russia." Marx and Engels, *Letters to Americans,* International Publishers, 1953, pp. 80-81.

3. The monarchists in France were at that time divided into three parties: the Legitimists—adherents of the "legitimate" dynasty of the Bourbons; the Orleanists—adherents of the Orleans dynasty; and the Bonapartists—adherents of Louis Bonaparte.

4. The *coup d'etat* of Louis Bonaparte by which he made himself Emperor. *See* Marx, *The Eighteenth Brumaire of Louis Bonaparte,* International Publishers, 1963.

5. The Second Empire in France was the name given to the period of the rule of Louis Bonaparte (Napoleon III, 1852-70) in distinction to the First Empire of Napoleon I (1804-14).

6. The war with Austria was contrived by Bismarck in order to get rid of Prussia's old competitor in the unification of Germany. Prussia conquered Austria in this war and so secured the hegemony in German unification. Napoleon III remained neutral in the Austro-Prussian War because he hoped to receive as a reward part of the territory of the German states, as promised him by Bismarck.

7. At Sedan (a town in northeast France) on September 2, 1870, the bulk of the French army, headed by the emperor, surrendered to the German troops.

8. The mobile National Guard—reserve troops created by Napoleon III in 1868 for protection of the towns in case of war.

9. For the purpose of municipal administration, Paris was divided into *arrondissements,* each of which had a mayor at the head.

10. Louis XVI was executed during the first French bourgeois revolution (on January 21, 1793).

11. The split in the French Workers' Party, into the supporters of Brousse (Possibilists), and the supporters of Guesde (Marxists), took place at the congress in Etienne in 1882. The opportunist wing, the Possibilists or Broussists, who were hunting for electoral victories, repudiated the party programme, restricting themselves in their agitation solely to "realisable" demands; they fought against party discipline, demanding autonomy for the local organisations in the question of the election platform and in the tactic of blocs with other parties.

12. At an earlier period the Democratic Party represented principally the interests of the landowning South, while the Republican Party represented the interests of the industrial North.

13. In all editions published previous to 1932 the text had the words "the German philistine." This was a falsification. Engels' manuscript, in the possession of the Institute of Marxism-Leninism in Moscow, has the words "the Social-Democratic philistine." The phrase "Social-Democratic" was afterwards crossed out (not by Engels) and the word "German" inserted in an unknown handwriting.

14. The plebiscite was arranged by Napoleon III in order to consolidate his empire and undermine republican agitation in the country. On May 8, 1870, the nation was to express its attitude to certain of the government's liberal reforms and amendments introduced into the constitution. Voting for the new constitution, and consequently for the empire, were 7,358,786 persons, against 1,571,939, while 1,894,681 abstained.

15. This refers to the third court prosecution against the International taking place under the empire.

16. The war between France and Germany began on July 19, 1870.

17. *See* Marx, *The Eighteenth Brumaire of Louis Bonaparte*, p. 75.

18. On the German side, the war was a war of defence in so far as it was directed against Bonapartist France, which was interested in the dismemberment of Germany and hindered German unification (national unity was a basic question for the German bourgeois revolution). While giving this characterisation of the war, Marx and Engels at the same time demanded from the German Workers' Party that it should: (1) sharply distinguish between German national and Prussian dynastic interests; (2) oppose the annexation of Alsace-Lorraine; (3) make peace as soon as a republican, non-chauvinist government came to power in Paris; (4) unceasingly emphasise the unity of German and French workers, who did not approve of the war and had no quarrel with one another.

19. The battle at Sadowa (in Bohemia) on July 3, 1886, played a decisive role in the Austro-Prussian war. After the Prussian victory over Austria, the latter was excluded from the German Federation and an important part of

Bismarck's plan for the unification of Germany was accomplished (the creation of the North German Confederation).

20. On the French side, the war was a dynastic one; Louis Bonaparte hoped by victory over the foreign foe to be able to save the crumbling edifice of the Bonapartist Empire.

21. Germany conducted the war against Napoleon I in alliance with tsarist Russia. By means of the "Holy Alliance," created after the victory over Napoleon I (1814–15), Russia attained a tremendous influence in international politics and began to play the role of "the gendarme of Europe." Prussia, as Marx expressed it, became "the fifth wheel of the coach of the European states."

22. The French army was heavily defeated at Sedan on September 2 and the emperor taken prisoner. On September 4, the republic was proclaimed in France and the so-called "Government of National Defence" set up.

23. By the Treaty of Tilsit (1807) France compelled Prussia to reduce the army, to pay a war indemnity of 100 million talers and to surrender territory in the west and east.

24. In 1865, Louis Bonaparte promised Bismarck France's neutrality in case of an Austro-Prussian war. In 1870, the Russian Foreign Minister Gorchakov promised Russia's neutrality in a Franco-Prussian war.

25. The Russian press attacked the Russian government for its friendly attitude toward Prussia.

26. The basis for this manifesto was Marx's letter of instructions to the committee of the German Social-Democratic Party (published in the *Volkstaat*, September 11, 1871).

27. In regard to this, *see* Lenin's Preface to Marx, *Letters to Dr. Kugelmann*, in this volume.

28. Marx has in mind the wave of national feeling among the masses in France in 1792 during the struggle with the attacking armies of the coalition of European states. He warns against a mechanical application of the slogan "the fatherland in danger" to the Franco-Prussian war. "To fight the Prussians on behalf of the bourgeoisie would be madness." (Engels.)

29. At the presidential election (December 10, 1848) Louis Bonaparte exploited the prejudices of the French peasants; they gave him their votes in recollection of Napoleon Bonaparte with whose name they erroneously associated the achievements of the first French bourgeois revolution.

30. Marx has in mind the great campaign of meetings, which developed in England on the initiative of Marx and the General Council of the International, for securing recognition of the French republic.

31. The war conducted by the first coalition of the powers (Austria, Prussia, Sardinia, etc.) against the first French bourgeois revolution. In February 1793, England and Holland, and in March, Spain also joined in the war.

32. During the Civil War in America (1861–65) between the industrial

North and the slave South, the English bourgeoisie supported the South, i.e., slavery. This was due to the fact that the English bourgeoisie saw a growing rival in the industrial North, while the South represented a supplier of cotton for the English market.

33. The ferocious suppression in Paris in 1839 of the rising of the Society for the Rights of Man during which unarmed persons, including women and children, were slaughtered.

34. Ferdinand II of Naples was given the nickname of King Bomba for his furious bombardment of Palermo and Messina, September 1848, to suppress the revolution.

35. This refers to the suppression of the June insurrection of the Paris proletariat in 1848.

36. Don Carlos (1545–68). Spanish prince who took part in the conspiracy against his father. He is idealised by Schiller in the latter's tragedy, *Don Carlos*.

37. The chief historical works of Thiers are: *History of the French Revolution* and *History of the Consulate and the Empire*.

38. The French system of protection was marked by high import duties on commodities (*e.g.*, the duty on English cast-iron was 70 per cent of its value, that on iron 105 per cent of its value). As a result, many tools and other commodities which could not be produced in France vanished altogether from the market.

39. The Chamber of Deputies in France, which consisted mainly of extreme monarchists, representatives of the nobility, and was marked by its reactionary character.

40. The National Assembly which opened in Bordeaux on February 13 had a majority of outspoken royalists (450 out of 750 deputies), chiefly representatives of the landowners. Hence its name of Assembly of "Rurals."

41. Cayenne, capital of French Guiana in South America, notorious penal settlement.

42. His function was to serve imprisonment if the newspaper was prosecuted.

43. On October 31, 1870, an attempt was made to overthrow the Government of National Defence and to seize power. The impulse for the movement was provided by rumours of an armistice about to be concluded with the Prussians, of the defeat of the National Guard at Le Bourget (October 30) and of the capitulation of Metz. Led by Blanquists, a battalion of National Guards composed chiefly of workers, occupied the Town Hall, proclaimed the overthrow of the old government and the establishment of a new one which would organise elections to the Commune. The new government, which did not base itself on the masses, proved irresolute and vacillating. It entered into negotiations with the arrested members of the Government of National Defence and obtained from them a verbal promise to

institute elections for the Commune (on November 1) and to declare a general amnesty. In the meantime, battalions of the Civil Guard were concentrated at the Town Hall and on the morning of November 1, they occupied it and restored the Government of National Defence to power.

44. On January 22, 1871, a new attempt was made to overthrow the Government of National Defence. The immediate occasion for this attempt was the defeat of the National Guard at Bougainville (January 10, 1871), rumours of an armistice and the appointment of General Vinoy as military governor of Paris. The attempt of January 22, like that of October 31, was marked by lack of determination and unity, and absence of organisational contact with the masses. During its suppression, thirty persons were killed or wounded, including women and children.

45. About these fatal mistakes of the Central Committee, Marx wrote to Kugelmann on April 12, 1871. *See* pp. 86*f* in this volume.

46. Marx here formulates one of the fundamental lessons of the Paris Commune. The tremendous significance attached by Marx and Engels to this lesson is evident from their remarks in the Preface to *The Communist Manifesto*, dated June 24, 1872. There it is said that the Programme of *The Communist Manifesto* has "in some details become antiquated. One thing especially," they continue, "was proved by the Commune, *viz.*, that 'the working class cannot simply lay hold of the ready-made state machinery and wield it for its own purposes.' . . ." For the full Preface, *see* Marx and Engels, *Selected Works* (one-volume edition), International Publishers, 1968. The same sentence is retained by Engels in his Introduction of 1888 (*The Communist Manifesto*, International Publishers, 1948, p. 7).

47. The wars waged by England, Russia, Prussia, Austria, Spain and other states against revolutionary France and later against the empire of Napoleon I.

48. Refers to the Bonapartist empire.

49. In connection with this characterisation of the Commune as a new type of state, *see* Lenin's comments, pp. 105*ff* of this volume.

50. In regard to this characterisation of parliamentarism, *see* Lenin, pp. 113*ff* in this volume.

51. The Girondins were the party of the industrial and commercial bourgeoisie during the epoch of the first French bourgeois revolution. Wishing to behead the revolution and to weaken the centralisation of revolutionary forces, they endeavoured to convert France into a Federation and to destroy the leading role of revolutionary Paris.

52. For Lenin's analysis of the historical importance of the lessons derived from the Commune by Marx, *see* especially pp. 121*ff* in this volume.

53. The Central Committee of the National Guard as late as March 20 had postponed payment on bills of exchange until October 1, 1871. On April 18, the Commune promulgated a decree postponing payments on debt obligations for three years.

54. Free-thinking—hostile to the priests and the church.

55. The Bourbon dynasty, which was restored to power after the overthrow of Napoleon I, decided to compensate the French nobility for the land taken from it during the first French bourgeois revolution. One billion francs was paid to the nobility.

56. The 45-centime tax was introduced in 1848 by the bourgeois provisional government with the object of creating dissension between the proletariat and the peasantry. The government gave as the reason for the tax the necessity of feeding the workers. The increase of taxation on the peasants by almost 50 per cent turned the peasantry against the revolution and the republic.

57. The Party of Order during the 1848 Revolution united the royalist big bourgeoisie and the landowners.

58. Alsace and Lorraine.

59. During the Second Empire, Baron Haussmann was Prefect of the Department of the Seine, i.e., of the City of Paris. He caused a number of new streets and buildings to be constructed.

60. In the church of St. Laurent were discovered skeletons of women who had been violated by the monks and buried alive in the vaults. In the Picpus nunnery women were held on the pretext that they were insane, and they suffered the same fate.

61. Irish landlords who squandered their "income" outside the country, hardly ever visiting their estates.

62. The tennis court where in 1789 the National Assembly took an oath not to dissolve, in spite of the royal command, before the constitution had been drafted.

63. The centre of the counter-revolutionary nobility in emigration during the first French bourgeois revolution.

64. De Calonne was Comptroller General (a kind of Prime Minister) in France on the eve of the 1789 Revolution.

65. The outbreak of the revolution and proclamation of the Commune in Lyons occurred on March 22, and in Marseilles on March 23; both were quickly crushed by the Thiers government. The Commune was also proclaimed in Toulouse, Narbonne, St. Etienne and some other towns.

66. By the commercial treaty with England concluded by Napoleon III in 1860, duties on English goods were lowered.

67. This letter was first published in *Neue Zeit*, XX-1, 1901–02, p. 709. For Lenin's comment, *see* his introduction to *Letters to Dr. Kugelmann*, pp. 91ff in this volume. Ludwig Kugelmann (1830–1902), a physician and a German Social-Democrat, took part in the German Revolution of 1848 and became a member of the First International. From 1862 to 1874, he corresponded with Marx, informing him of events in Germany.

68. Lenin's explanation of why Marx restricted his conclusion to the

Continent, will be found in the excerpt from *State and Revolution*, p. 107 in this volume.

69. For Lenin's summary of the mistakes of the Commune, *see* his introduction to the *Letters to Dr. Kugelmann*, in this volume.

70. *See* Marx, *The Class Struggles in France, 1848–50*, Chap. III. International Publishers, 1964.

71. Jules Favre (1809–1880), bourgeois republican and member of Government of National Defence (1870), took part in the bloody suppression of the Paris Commune. *See* Marx's references to him in the Addresses.

72. Etienne Cabet (1788–1856), French utopian Communist, author of *Travels in Icaria*.

73. Jean–Baptiste Millière (1817–1871), Left follower of Proudhon who participated in the Commune and was shot by the Versaillists, May 26, 1871 by orders of Jules Favre. For the documents published by him, *see* p. 38 in this volume.

74. Appended to the pamphlet, was a further note, as follows: "In an article on 'The International Society and Its Aims,' that pious informer, the London *Spectator* (June 24th), among other similar tricks, quotes, even more fully than Jules Favre has done, the above document of the 'Alliance' as the work of the International, and that eleven days after the refutation had been published in the *Times*. We do not wonder at this. Frederick the Great used to say that of all Jesuits the worst are the Protestant ones."

NOTES FOR PART TWO

1. An excerpt from V. I. Lenin's preface to Karl Marx, *Letters to Dr. Kugelmann*, the first Russian edition of which appeared in 1907 (*Novaya Duma* Publishers, St. Petersburg). The book was edited by Lenin.

2. Georgy V. Plekhanov (1856–1918), considered the founder of Marxism in Russia, went over to the Mensheviks in 1903. The reference to December 1905 is to the armed uprising of the workers in Moscow, where extensive barricade fighting took place. For Lenin's articles on the Moscow uprising and the Revolution of 1905, *see* V. I. Lenin, *Selected Works* (3 vols.), International Publishers, 1967, Vol. I.

3. *See* Marx's "*Second Address*," in the present book, pp. 28*ff*.

4. *Proudhonists and Blanquists.* Pierre–Joseph Proudhon (1809–1865), French economist and ideologue of the petty bourgeoisie, was one of the founders of anarchism. Louis Auguste Blanqui (1805–1881), a French revolutionary and Utopian communist, emphasized conspiratorial methods by small groups. He was a leader of the Commune.

5. *See* p. 86 of the present volume.

6. "The Man in a Muffler," the central character in a story of that name by Anton Chekhov, is a limited, philistine type who fears all initiative and everything new.

7. This and the two previous quotations are from the letter to Kugelmann, April 12, 1871, in this volume, p. 86.

8. *Cadets.* Abbreviated for Constitutional-Democratic Party, the chief political party of the liberal-monarchist bourgeoisie in Russia, formed in 1905.

9. *See* p. 86 of present volume.

10. Letter to Kugelmann, April 17, 1871. *See* p. 87 of this book.

11. The article "Lessons of the Commune" appeared in *Zagranichnaya Gazeta (Foreign Gazette)*, a newspaper published by a group of Russian emigrants in Geneva, No. 2, March 23, 1908. It is a verbatim report of a speech made by Lenin. The editors of the newspaper introduced the article with the following remarks: "An international meeting was held in Geneva on March 18 to commemorate three proletarian anniversaries: the twenty-fifth anniversary of the death of Marx, the sixtieth anniversary of the March revolution of 1848, and the anniversary of the Paris Commune. Comrade Lenin on behalf of the Russian Social-Democratic Labour Party spoke at the meeting on the significance of the Commune."

12. *See* this volume, pp. 28*ff*.

13. In the Manifesto, the tsar, frightened by the revolution, promised the people civil liberties and a constitution.

14. This article appeared in *Rabochaya Gazeta* (Workers' Gazette), No. 4–5, April 15, 1911.

15. Tsarist generals, notorious for their brutal punitive actions during the 1905–07 Revolution in Russia.

16. This excerpt consists of the entire Chapter III of Lenin's *State and Revolution* (International Publishers, 1943). The reader is advised to read that entire work in which Lenin develops his theoretical conclusions.

17. *See* Note 46 to Part I.

18. *See* Chapter VI of *State and Revolution.*

19. In Chapter II of *State and Revolution,* on "The Experiences of 1848–1851."

20. Pyotr B. Struve (1870–1944), a bourgeois economist who was the leading representative of "legal Marxism" in the 1890's, and later became a leader of the Cadets.

21. *See* pp. 54–57 in this volume.

22. *See* pp. 57–58 in this volume.

23. Eduard Bernstein (1850–1932), leader of the opportunist wing of the German Social-Democracy; he emerged as the ideologist of revisionism in 1896–98 when he published a series of articles, "Problems of Socialism," in which he opposed the basic revolutionary tenets of Marxism.

24. Followers of Karl Kautsky (1854–1938), one of the leaders and theoreticians of the German Social-Democracy and of the Second International; a "Centrist" who later opposed the Soviet Union.

25. *See* p. 60 in this volume.

26. *See* pp. 57, 59 in this volume.

27. Lenin is referring to the government set up in Russia after the bourgeois-democratic revolution of March 1917.

28. *See* pp. 58–59 in this volume.

29. An English translation was published under the title *Evolutionary Socialism.* The quotations that follow are translated anew from the German edition, 1899, pp. 134–136.

30. Mikhail A. Bakunin (1814–1876), Russian revolutionary anarchist theoretician who was expelled from the First International at the Hague Congress in 1872 for his divisive activities.

31. *See* pp. 59–60 in this volume.

32. *See* p. 60 in this volume.

33. Excerpt from a speech delivered at the Seventh Congress of the Russian Communist Party, on the Revision of the Programme and the Name of the Party. The Congress took place March 6–8, 1918.

34. Excerpt from "Theses and Report on Bourgeois Democracy and the

Dictatorship of the Proletariat," presented to the First Congress of the Communist International, March 2–6, 1919.

35. Excerpts from "Task of the Proletariat in our Revolution" (known as the "April Theses"), written April 10, 1917, and first published as a pamphlet in September 1917. It is published in full in Lenin, *Selected Works* (3 vols.), Vol. II.

36. In a letter to August Bebel, German Social-Democratic leader, March 18–28, 1875, published in *The Selected Correspondence of Karl Marx and Frederick Engels, 1846–1895*, International Publishers, 1942, p. 332.

37. In the Address on the Civil War in France; see p. 60 of this book.

MARX'S "Civil War in France"
by Nikita Fedorovsky

MARX'S "Civil War in France"
by Nikita Fedorovsky

CONTENTS

Translated from the Russian by Dudley Hagen

Karl Marx's *The Civil War in France* is not a voluminous work; it occupies some sixty-odd printed pages. The time spent on its writing was not lengthy either, being about equal to the time for which the Paris Commune endured. Nonetheless, *The Civil War in France* occupies a position of importance and honour in the treasure-house of Marxist theoretical thought.

Marx considered the actions of the broad popular masses to be one of the prime movers in historical development. Such actions take on particular significance at times when radical shifts and changes are going on in society, when major revolutionary shocks are being felt. Marx regarded the experience accumulated by the working people in their mass actions as material of the highest value for the development of the theory of proletarian revolution. A vast portion of his writings is devoted to the analysis of such experience. The approach is always highly concrete. Marx never regarded the people—the protagonist in any revolution—as an abstract, homogeneous mass. In each individual case, he clearly perceived the deployment of class forces, and also the level of development attained by each class and its role and place in society. In the words of Vladimir Ilyich Lenin, the founder of the Soviet state, "Marx's method consists, first of all, in taking due account of the *objective* content of a historical process...in definite and concrete conditions."[1] Marx always had a clear idea of the objective and subjective causes behind the mass movement under consideration and of the practical aims that shaped it.

It was the bourgeoisie that reaped the principal benefits from the revolutionary activities of the popular masses in the eighteenth century and the first half of the nineteenth. This was so because the main goal of bourgeois revolutions is to do away with the remnants of feudal society, which hinder progress. Up to a certain time, this corresponded to the interests of most working people as well, and thus the bourgeoisie was legitimately able to assume leadership in anti-feudal revolutionary movements.

At the same time as the bourgeoisie was gathering influence and power, however, the antagonist destined to vanquish it—the working class—was also growing stronger. Working people were no longer content with the slogans of the bourgeoisie, which were still being proclaimed in the name of society as a whole. At the time of the European revolutions of 1848-1849, the proletariat came forward with its own demands. The most memorable example was the rising of workers in Paris in June of 1848. For three days the red banner waved on the barricades in the French capital. For three days the workers of the Paris suburbs fought to the death against heavily armed, superior forces. The first battle of the French proletariat against capitalist society ended in defeat for the workers. The enraged bourgeoisie inflicted fierce repressions as vengeance for the fright it had suffered. Thousands of the rebels were summarily shot, sent off to hard labour, or condemned to an early death from tropical fevers in overseas French colonies. In the memory of the international proletariat, the June rebellion remained as a prologue to the Paris Commune.

From this moment on, Marx regarded studying the practical experience of the working class and building generalisations on it as one of his most important theoretical aims. He drew lessons for the future from the proletariat's defeats no less than from its victories. Marx's theory was not the result of abstract thought, but of generalisation and painstaking analysis of reality, of the development of the class struggle. This was the principal reason for its profoundly scientific character. Lenin wrote: "There is not trace of utopianism in Marx, in the sense that he made up or invented a 'new' society. No, he studied the *birth* of the new society *out of* the old, and the forms of transition from the latter to the former, as a natural-historical process. He examined the actual experience of a mass proletarian movement and tried to draw practical lessons from it. He 'learned' from the Commune, just as all the great revolutionary thinkers learned unhesitatingly from the experience of great movements of the oppressed classes."[2]

The Paris Commune gave Marx a unique opportunity to witness at first hand the rise, development, and defeat of the first proletarian revolution in history, and the only one in the nineteenth century. The main object of his study *The Civil War in France* was the activities of the aroused revolutionary masses of Paris, headed by the working class. Marx followed these activities with great interest and undisguised admiration. He paid particular attention to the Parisians' spontaneous efforts to organise themselves in their struggle for the further development of the revolution. While giving due regard to revolutionary enthusiasm and the selflessness of the working people of Paris, he was far from overestimating the part that such unpremeditated outbreaks by the popular masses play in the class struggle. The tragedy of the Communards showed what enormous significance organisational and ideological unity in the ranks of the proletariat has for its victory. This unity can be provided only by a cohesive proletarian party, armed with a scientific theory.

For Marx, the Paris Commune was more than just confirmation of one of his central theses, the dictatorship of the proletariat. In *The Civil War in France* he showed that the dictatorship of the proletariat is not a speculative construct born in the quiet studies of theorising scholars, but a predictable result of the revolutionary creativity of the broad proletarian masses. In the two months it existed, the working-class government in Paris convincingly demonstrated the truth of Marx's idea that the power of the proletariat organically expresses the interests of all the exploited.

As if foreseeing the attempts later made by falsifiers of the theory of proletarian revolution to advance a distorted concept of the dictatorship of the proletariat and frighten ordinary people with the horror of a dictatorial totalitarian regime maintained by a narrow group of professional revolutionaries, Marx presented, in *The Civil War in France*, irrefutable facts by which he showed that the emergence of the working class as the dominant force in society marks a new and higher stage in the development of democracy, in which democracy for the chosen few becomes democracy for the majority. The idea of transforming the power of the state from a weapon used by a few exploiters to oppress and hold down the popular masses into an instrument for the political and economic liberation of the people is one of the keystones of *The Civil War in France*.

* * *

The renowned work by Marx being considered here, like any other scientific treatise, should be approached concretely and historically. This means that the work as a whole, the tasks it sets for itself, its significance, and the individual problems it deals with are to be considered from the standpoint of the historical conditions, place, and time in which it was written. It is especially important to take into consideration the overall historical situation, the proletariat's level of organisation and self-awareness at that time, the state of the working-class movement in Europe and in France, and the degree of development and forms of the class struggle. Such an approach makes it possible to comprehend more deeply the purposes of Marx's work, its distinctive features and significance, and to arrive at a fuller interpretation of the ideas put forward and vindicated in it.

An acquaintance with other landmarks of Marxist theory, such as *The Class Struggles in France* and *The Eighteenth Brumaire of Louis Bonaparte,* is of considerable help in understanding *The Civil War in France* more fully and deeply. In these works Marx showed the class basis of the regime of Napoleon III, revealed its adventuristic character, and foretold the inevitable downfall of the empire of "the little nephew of a great uncle."

In order to see yet again the accuracy of prediction characteristic of Marx's thought, we may turn to the "Address of the Central Authority to the League" written by Marx and Engels in March of 1850. In this document the founders of scientific communism, in working out the tactics of the proletariat in a bourgeois revolution, anticipated the forms of working-class organisation in the course of a revolutionary struggle that were spontaneously created twenty years later by the working people of Paris.

The conclusions at which Marx arrived in *The Civil War in France* were further developed in the works of Engels and Lenin, especially in *The*

*Housing Question** and *On Authority,* written by Engels in 1873, and in his introduction to the third German edition of *The Civil War in France.*** Great benefit is undoubtedly to be derived from studying the method Lenin used in his work with *The Civil War in France* while preparing to write *The State and Revolution.*

---

*Marx/Engels, *Collected Works* 23:317-391
**pp. 9-22, this book

On July 19, 1870, France declared war on Prussia. The *casus belli* was a dispute over the vacant throne of Spain. A bourgeois revolution had begun in Spain in 1868, and Queen Isabella II had fled the country. The Constituent Cortes (assembly) that met in February of 1869 adopted a constitution retaining the monarchy in Spain, and the provisional government began looking around for a new king. Leopold von Hohenzollern, a prince related to the ruling dynasty of Prussia, was offered the crown and accepted, but the French government vigorously opposed his candidacy. The rulers of the Second Empire viewed the situation as a convenient excuse for bringing about an international crisis and provoking an armed conflict. The Prussian government sought the same end, and with equal energy.

The causes for this militant hostility were, of course, far more serious than the question of who would inherit the Spanish throne. In the late 1860s and early 1870s, the process by which centralised bourgeois national governments were formed in Europe was reaching completion. The ruling groups in the European countries strove to prevent this problem from being solved from below, through popular revolutions. They preferred to achieve national unity by redistributing power within the exploiter classes, through dynastic wars. In this the ruling elite of Prussia was no exception.

Prince Otto von Bismarck, a representative of the reactionary landowners, had become head of the Prussian government in 1862. He was one of the outstanding political leaders of his time. Possessed of an exceptional intellect and a will of iron, he was completely unscrupulous in attaining his ends, of which he declared the unification of Germany through "blood and iron" to be the greatest. Victories in wars against Denmark (1864) and Austria (1866) ensured Prussia's leadership in the struggle to unify the country. The North German Confederation was established in 1867, at Bismarck's initiative; it included twenty-two German states. Prussia naturally played the dominant role in its governing bodies.

By 1870, only one obstacle remained in the way of unifying Germany under the aegis of the Hohenzollerns (the ruling dynasty of Prussia): the Second Empire of Napoleon III. The French ruler had been of considerable help to the Prussian government in its quest for hegemony over the German lands, and Bismarck had learned a good deal from his crafty and treacherous neighbour. But, by the beginning of the seventies, the days of unclouded relations between the two chief European predators were long past. The leaders of the Second Empire saw the final unification of Germany as a serious threat to themselves. They were not at all pleased by the appearance of a strong, centralised state on France's northern border.

Louis Napoleon Bonaparte, the nephew of Napoleon I, had come to power on December 2, 1851, as the result of a coup. The Second Empire had its chief social support among the well-to-do peasantry. It also had the active support of the Catholic clergy and the French military. In essence, however, the regime of Louis Bonaparte was an expression of the interests of the bourgeoisie controlling high finance. The power of the banks increased rapidly under it, and the Paris stock market became one of the most important financial centres in Europe. Capital began to be exported. Napoleon III and his associates resorted to the most shameless social demagoguery in order to tighten their grip on power, trying to make it seem that the Second Empire stood above parties and classes, that it defended the interests of the whole French people. In actual fact, Louis Bonaparte put the finishing touches to a monstrous governmental apparatus for repression and did away with most of the democratic gains made in earlier years. All revolutionary and working-class organisations were mercilessly persecuted.

The ruling elite of the Second Empire proved incapable of resolving the acute class conflicts. While the big-business bourgeoisie grew richer, the masses of working people were reduced to destitution. The exploitation of workers became more galling, and the increase in large-scale production hastened the ruin of tradesmen and small shop owners. Most of the peasantry had too little land, and suffered from high taxes, and browbeating by the police. The venality of civil servants reached unprecedented proportions; the Emperor himself sanctioned and was involved in many financial schemes.

In an attempt to distract the masses from problems within the country, Napoleon III pursued continual predatory and colonial wars. Many of these costly ventures ended in disgraceful failures. Relations between France and most of her European neighbours suffered serious damage. By the end of the sixties, the Second Empire was unmistakably in crisis. There were miscarriages in foreign policy, and at the same time class conflicts within the country became more acute. The anti-Bonapartists grew more numerous and powerful. The French government hoped to avert the oncoming political catastrophe by rushing into yet another military adventure. It was not long before a suitable occasion turned up.

The ruling classes in France and Germany were also hoping that an armed conflict could be used to emasculate the working-class movement, the growth of which was causing serious concern among reactionaries throughout Europe.

The European bourgeoisie saw the First International as the greatest threat. The International Working Men's Association (as the organisation was officially known) was founded on September 28, 1864, at an international meeting convened in London by British and French workers. Representatives of the Polish, Italian, and German proletariat also took part. Among those present was Karl Marx.

At the first meeting Marx was elected to membership in the General Council; it was he who composed the founding documents of the first international mass organisation of the proletariat. He and Engels (who began to participate actively in the work of the International soon after) exerted an enormous influence on the development of the International Working Men's Association. Its headquarters were set up in London, which at that time offered the most bearable conditions for various types of democratic and working-class organisations. The headquarters had ties with local sections in other countries, which often arose on the basis of existing working-class groups.

The principal task of the International was to develop a sense of proletarian internationalism in the workers of different countries. There was a need to help the proletariat in Europe and the USA realise its common interests, to teach it to think of itself as a single whole and act as such.

To achieve this, the programmatic documents of the International Working Men's Association formulated the organisation's basic demands in a way that would be acceptable to workers with different views and theoretical backgrounds. At the same time, however, Marx and Engels were striving to imbue the consciousness of the proletariat's most advanced member's with the fundamentals of scientific communism. The principles of Marxist theory were upheld in a hard struggle against the adherents of petty-bourgeois trends within the working-class movement: the reformist and the followers of the anarchist theoreticians Proudhon and Bakunin. It was life itself that arbitrated the dispute between Marxism and the socialist doctrines that opposed it. The influence of a given theoretical conception was determined by its ability to supply a correct answer to the urgent questions that the unfolding class struggle put before the international proletariat.

The practical work of the International Working Men's Association was of great significance in the revolutionary education of the proletariat. Solidarity between various contingents of the working class in Europe and the USA was forged during its actions in support of the strike movement. The participation of the International in the general democratic campaigns of that time (giving support to the Polish and Irish peoples in their fight for independence, and opposing interference by the British government in the American Civil War) helped the more advanced workers to understand the close connection between the proletariat's class struggle and the solution of current democratic and national problems. Many of the leaders of the working-class movement educated in the ranks of the International Working Men's Association went on to play an important role in creating national proletarian parties.

The activities of the First International provoked fear and hatred among all of the international bourgeoisie and in reactionary circles. In the imagination of the bourgeois frightened by the "red menace" the International was a monstrous octopus enveloping the whole world, the instigator of most disturbances and troubles. Ideas about the power of the International Working Men's Association were often overblown, and officialdom helped to fan the flames. In an attempt to justify repressive measures against the working-class movement, the governments of several European countries declared that the International was a secret conspiratorial society, guided by the sinister London centre headed by Marx. The bourgeois and reactionary press of Europe seized on these fabrications and elaborated them in every possible way. The persecution that resulted from these horror stories was perfectly tangible: members of the International Working Men's Association were refused jobs, organisations in Germany were threatened with disbandment for allying themselves with it, and in Austria-Hungary and France legal actions were brought against local sections of the International.

The policy of Napoleon III on the labour issue was characteristically contradictory, demagogic, and reactionary. He flirted with the French proletariat and posed as a defender of working people's interests. This was the purpose behind certain measures adopted by the government of the Second Empire in the sixties. The law forbidding strikes was repealed; public meetings were permitted (although with severe restrictions); *syndicats* (professional organisations) were legalised; and police censorship of the press was relaxed somewhat. But these half-measures could not halt the growth of the working-class movement in the country. Once they saw that their attempt to bring the proletariat to heel had failed, the French ruling elite resorted once again to overt repression, aimed principally at the country's sections of the International Working Men's Association.

The first sections had appeared in 1864; several years later, they had become a real political force. The government of Louis Bonaparte was particularly worried by the ties between French members of the International and the working-class movement in other European countries, and their part in organising the strike movement. It was also frightened by the increasingly revolutionary mood in the ranks of the French sections of the International Working Men's Association. The moderate followers of Proudhon, a petty-bourgeois socialist theoretician who called for a peaceful, utopian solution of the conflict between capital and labour, were replaced by new people who moved further and further away from Proudhon's basic dogmas, even though they continued to consider themselves his disciples. They set aside reverence for private property and faith in the magical power of the co-operative movement and took an active part in creating professional organisations and directing strikes; they entirely rejected the Napoleonic regime and were ready to enter into overt opposition to it. A number of the future leaders of the Paris Commune, such as Eugène Varlin, a bookbinder who became one of its heroes and martyrs, began to play a prominent role in the Paris sections of the International at this time.

The government of the Second Empire subjected the French organisations of the International Working Men's Association to police persecution. In 1868, two legal actions were brought against leading figures in the International in Paris. They were fined and sentenced to prison. The sections of the International Working Men's Association were declared disbanded. They went underground, but did not abandon their activities. In the summer of 1870, legal action against the International was taken for a third time. Thirty-eight persons were accused, and the sentence was passed two weeks before the start of the Franco-Prussian war.

The fears of the international bourgeoisie proved well grounded. The results of the work done by the International Working Men's Association made themselves felt in the very first days of the war. Both in France and in Germany, the vanguard of the proletariat declared unanimous opposition to the blood-letting and spurned the feelings of national hatred being promoted by chauvinists.

The General Council of the First International issued an address, written by Karl Marx, to all the Association's members. It declared that the aims of the fratricidal Franco-Prussian War unleashed by Napoleon III were contrary to the interests of the French proletariat. Marx pointed out that Louis Bonaparte and his associates needed the war to keep them in power and said that the "war plot of July, 1870" was "an amended edition of the *coup d'etat* of December, 1851." [3] He continued prophetically: "Whatever may be the incidents of Louis Bonaparte's war with Prussia, the death knell of the Second Empire has already sounded at Paris. It will end as it began, by a parody." While noting that the war, in its present stage, was a defensive one for Germany, Marx noted at the same time that it was "the governments and the ruling classes of Europe who enabled Louis Bonaparte to play during eighteen years the ferocious farce of the *Restored Empire*. [4] The contribution of the Prussian ruling circles had been especially great. Marx called on German workers to keep the conflict with France from turning into a predatory war of conquest.

Marx welcomed the courageous opposition to the war by representatives of the International in France and Germany. In the name of the British proletariat, he expressed the deep conviction that "whatever turn the impending horrid war may take, the alliance of the working classes of all countries will ultimately kill war." For Marx the feelings of proletarian solidarity and internationalism that were manifested in France and Germany were a "great fact" that "opens the vista of a brighter future. It proves that in contrast to old society, with its economic miseries and its political delirium, a new society is springing up, whose international rule will be *peace,* because its national ruler will be everywhere the same—*Labour!*"[5] Events confirmed the correctness of the basic appraisals and conclusions of this address. The very first battles showed the German forces to be greatly superior. The disintegration of the Second Empire's police apparatus and bureaucracy was mirrored in the utter unpreparedness for combat of the French army.

France entered the war practically without allies. The mobilisation was very poorly conducted, and the confusion was increased by the failure of railways to operate properly and by disarray among the various commands. As a result, the French army was unable to achieve sufficient troop concentration at the border for the opening of the war. The units mobilised were not adequately equipped. The Second Empire's war ministry, which had made preparations for action in Germany, had not even bothered to provide the officers with maps of French territory. Louis Napoleon's soldiers were armed with Chassepot rifles, which were technically superior to the weapons of the German army, but most of the French infantry had not been trained in the use of these modern firearms. The artillery that the French put into the field was significantly inferior to that of the Prussians. The German army, by making use of the weakness and oversights of the enemy, was able to secure a decisive numerical advantage in the main theatres of war.

Despite their undoubted courage, the French forces, under the command of incompetent Bonapartist generals, suffered one defeat after another. At the end of August 1870, the main force of the French army was soundly beaten and surrounded at the fortress of Sedan. On September 2, 83,000 French soldiers, with the Emperor himself at their head, surrendered. The way to the French capital was now open to the German forces.

The news of the capitulation of the Emperor's forces had no sooner reached Paris than Louis Bonaparte's Second Empire was overthrown by a revolution (September 4, 1870). The people demanded that a republic (the third in the history of France) be proclaimed. But the German forces continued to advance. There had now been a reversal of roles: republican France was struggling against an aggressor that threatened its very existence. The vanguard of the working class and of the democratically-minded public in Europe and the USA condemned the Prussian aggression, and demanded that a just peace be concluded with republican France. The General Council of the First International, in its second address on the Franco-Prussian War, called on the proletariat to give its full support to this demand. The appeal was written by Marx. He pointed out that Germany's war of defense had come to a close with "the surrender of Louis Bonaparte, the Sedan capitulation, and the proclamation of the Republic of Paris", [6] and went on to a devastating critique of the annexationist plans cherished by Germany's rulers. Marx showed that there was no basis for the claims of German chauvinists that certain French territories must be taken over to ensure the military security of the German state. "If limits are to be fixed by military interests," he wrote, "there will be no end to claims, because every military line is necessarily faulty, and may be improved by annexing some more outlying territory." He insightfully perceived that the flagrant robbery of the French people committed by Germany's ruling classes, drunk with their own impunity, would be the source of future wars in Europe. "History will measure its retribution, not by the extent of the square miles conquered from France," he warned, "but by the intensity of the crime of reviving, in the second half of the 19th century, *the policy of conquest!*"[7]

The appeal defined the tactics to be adopted by German and French workers in the new situation that arose after the downfall of the monarchy of Napoleon III. For the German proletariat, this meant working to end the war. Marx expressed the hope that "the German working class are not made of the same malleable stuff as the German middle class. They will do their duty."[8] The appeal laid special emphasis on the complexity of the situation in which the French proletariat now found itself. For the workers of France, the main task was to defend the motherland against the enemy at the gates of Paris. At the same time, Marx warned them of the dangers of falling victim to chauvinist propaganda, of being influenced by nationalistic traditions. He called on the French working class "not to recapitulate the past, but to build up the future."[9]

The first and second addresses of the General Council on the Franco-Prussian War constitute a sort of introduction to *The Civil War in France*. It was with good reason that Engels, preparing a third, commemorative German edition of Marx's celebrated work in 1891, included the two addresses along with it. He wrote in his introduction that the two addresses, like *The Civil War in France*, are "outstanding examples of the author's remarkable gift for grasping clearly the character, the import and the necessary consequences of great historical events, at a time when these events are still in progress before our eyes or have only just taken place."[10]

It was the people of Paris who brought about the revolution of September 4, 1870. But it was not able to enjoy the fruits of is victory. The proletariat of Paris—the only existing force that could have gathered the rest of the working people together in a struggle for power—proved incapable of accomplishing this at the critical moment. This was the consequence of the chauvinism of the early days of the war, and of a serious lack of organisation.

There was no group in Paris ready to head up the revolutionary masses of the city or to point out to them the chief goals and the means for their achievement. The Paris sections of the First International, weakened by the repressive measures of the last few months of the Second Empire and by serious disagreements within its own ranks, were unable to do it either.

The power in Paris fell into the hands of prótegés of the big-money bourgeoisie. Playing deftly on the critical state of the country (the enemy was approaching the capital), they set up a so-called Government of National Defence. This government, which Marx described as consisting "partly of notorious Orleanists (members of one of France's monarchist factions, supporters of the Orleans branch of the Valois and Bourbon dynasties that once ruled in France), partly of middle-class Republicans", had inherited from the Empire, not only ruins, but also its dread of the working class."[11] It was this fear that pushed the French ruling classes into outright betrayal of the national interest. While talking about "defending the motherland", the government was secretly moving towards capitulation. The popular masses of Paris, while knowing nothing of these intrigues, had an instinctive distrust of the authorities. All of their energies were devoted to organising a more effective resistance to the aggressors. The German forces reached the city's fortifications. The siege of Paris began on September 19, 1870. It lasted more than four months. Beginning in late December, the city came under heavy bombardment from German artillery. General Trochu, the head of the Government of National Defence and the military governor of Paris, and also his ministers did all they could to inculate the idea that it was impossible for Paris to resist any longer.

In addition to regular troops, there were sixty battalions of the National Guard defending Paris. They had been recruited in the days of the Second Empire from among the well-to-do citizens. The Government of National Defence was forced by popular pressure to allow the formation of 200 more battalions, which were made up mainly of Parisian workers. For the military command in Paris, working people organised and armed were an object of hatred and fear. The workers' battalions in the National Guard were not supplied with arms and ammunition, and were intentionally thrown into actions doomed to failure. Former Bonapartist officers were put in command of them in the place of their own chosen leaders.

The government did not concern itself with supplying the population of the besieged capital with fuel and foodstuffs. The factories and workshops stood idle. The smaller shops closed. Unemployment increased. Long queues formed outside bread stores long before dawn. Horse meat became a delicacy at the city markets; the meat of cats, dogs, and even rats was also sold. And in the midst of this sea of grief, deprivation, and poverty the money-bags continued to feast as usual in expensive restaurants, where tightly drawn

curtains concealed them from public view. The siege brought them no hard-
ships whatever. Indignation at the treachery of the bourgeois elite was
growing in the working-class districts of the city. The sabotage of the defence
by the government and its generals could not be concealed from the people
of Paris. To combat it successfully, the masses needed to unite and organise;
this had not yet been achieved by September 4, 1870. But the working people
of Paris, with the proletariat at their head, had the revolution to inspire
them; a brilliant flash of intuition showed them the way to victory. Mass
organisation was being accomplished in the period between September 1870
and March 18, 1871. Vigilance committees were set up in each district of the
city. Their mission was to supervise the actions of the authorities and to
prevent any sabotage of the defence. There was also a Central Committee,
which was made up of representatives from each of the twenty districts.
Numerous clubs openly opposing the government were also formed.

Although the Parisian sections of the International proved incapable of
heading up the revolutionary movement in the city, they played a very
important role in it. Members of the International Working Men's Association
took an active part in the creation and the work of most of the mass
organisations in Paris. The building in La Corderie Square where the Federal
Council of the Paris sections of the International met became one of the chief
revolutionary centres of the French capital. It became headquarters for the
city's trade unions, and was also the meeting-place of the Central Committee
of the Twenty Districts.

The responsibility of leading the working people of Paris in their fight
against reaction fell to the National Guard. This popular army achieved still
greater unity in the course of the struggle against the government's attempts
to gain control of it. Its military cohesion was amplified by political solidarity
in the early days of March 1871, when the Federation of the National Guard
was established. Its Central Committee, which was to lead the resistance of
the working masses against attempts to bring about a counter-revolution, was
set up just a few days before the revolution of March 18, 1871.

The social aspirations of the working people of Paris found expression in
the demand for the election of a municipal council, the Paris Commune. The
French capital had been deprived of its self-government under Napoleon I,
who well remembered the revolutionary Commune of the days of the bourgeois French revolution at the end of the eighteenth century. The centralisation of government power in a police and bureaucratic apparatus reached
its peak under the Second Empire.

For the broad masses, however, the Commune meant something more
than hope that the city's communal freedoms might be restored. They
expected it to bring about radical changes in the social structure, even if they
had as yet no very clear idea of what those changes might be. Two times, on

October 31, 1870, and on January 22, 1871, the working people of Paris tried to achieve by force the satisfaction of their chief demand. They were kept from success by their lack of cohesiveness and their weak organisation.

The growth of revolutionary feeling among the people of Paris frightened the French ruling classes. They hastened to make peace with Germany; a treaty was signed on January 28, 1871.

In February of 1871, elections for the country's National Assembly were held. Their result was determined by a number of objective factors. In the northern departments, the elections took place under the control of the German occupying forces. The peasantry, which made up most of the French population, was strongly influenced by the provincial bureaucracy and the clergy. The revolutionary ideas of Paris did not reach the rest of France, as the capital was isolated by the enemy blockade. The reactionaries made good use of the masses' disappointment at the loss of the war and their natural desire for peace. As a result, most of the National Assembly was made up of monarchists of all stripes, representatives of the so-called rustic faction, which embodied everything that was stagnant and conservative in French society. The government they formed was headed by Adolph Thiers, one of the most malicious and persistent enemies of the working class.

The preliminary peace agreement between France and Germany was signed on February 26, 1871, in Versailles. France conceded the greater part of Alsace and Lorraine to the victor, and agreed to pay a war indemnity of five thousand million francs. German forces were to remain on French territory until the ratification of the treaty by the National Assembly.

Now the French ruling circles could set about their main task: subduing revolutionary Paris. The Thiers government, on Bismarck's advice, tried to provoke the Parisians into armed action, which would then be ruthlessly suppressed. But the working people of the city retained their self-possession in the face of every attempt to do this. Then, in the early hours of March 18, 1871, regular troops made an effort to disarm the Parisian National Guard. Its artillery, which had been purchased with money contributed by the citizens themselves, was to be seized first. The working people of the capital had installed cannon on high ground commanding the city: Montmartre, Belleville, and Chaumont. The arms of the National Guardsmen were a serious threat to the plans of the reactionaries.

Sometime after two in the morning, the government's non-commissioned officers, without sounding any alarm, assembled their units. Columns of soldiers marched through the sleeping streets to the designated points of attack. Thiers's forces captured the cannon on Montmartre without any great difficulty, but were not able to remove them from the working-class districts of the city quickly enough. At dawn the inhabitants—mainly women who had set out to shop—began to crowd around the soldiers. The alarm was sounded. National Guardsmen rushed to their assembly points. The soldiers in the regular forces refused to obey the orders of their commanders and went over to the side of the people. The revolution in Paris had begun. At first, the proletariat thought only of defence, but the inescapable logic of battle soon forced it to move to the attack. In the afternoon of March 18, the Central Committee of the National Guard assumed command of the rebellion and sent its forces to seize the city's chief strategic points. By now the government forces were completely demoralised, and victory was achieved almost without bloodshed. Late in the evening the rebel forces seized the city hall and hoisted a red flag over it. Thiers and his generals fled to Versailles. The forces of the regular army were withdrawn to the same place, and government functionaries also made their way there. The Central Committee of the National Guard was now in control of the city. It was the first workers' government in history.

Paris celebrated the victory, which to most seemed complete and final. Only a few thought of the possibility that the civil war might continue. Instead of moving against Versailles to destroy the nest of counter-revolution that had formed there, the Central Committee of the National Guard proclaimed elections to the Paris Commune. The time lost made it possible for the Versailles government to reinforce its positions. This tragic mistake later proved fatal to the proletarian revolution in Paris.

Elections to the Commune were held on March 26. Most of its members represented the interests of the proletariat and the other classes of working people in the city. The largest faction in the Commune was made up of Blanquists and neo-Jacobins. The followers of Blanqui were determined and devoted revolutionaries, but had a poor understanding of the practical means by which the working class could be liberated. The group known as neo-Jacobins were the most consistent representatives of the petty-bourgeois democrats; they were dedicated republicans who continued the traditions of the Jacobins, the left wing of the bourgeois French revolution of the late eighteenth century.

Forty-one members of the International were elected to the Commune. Most of them belonged to one or another branch of the socialist school of Proudhon. The Commune had only two Marxists among its members. The Communards' unity of action was seriously hampered by the ideological diversity among the members of the first proletarian government, which diverted much time and energy to disagreements that could only do harm in the midst of a civil war.

Five days after the Paris Commune was proclaimed, the Versailles government began military operations against it. They were emboldened to do so only by the support of the ruling circles of the German empire. Bismarck ordered that French soldiers taken prisoner during the Franco-Prussian War be sent to Versailles. The collaboration of the German authorities made it possible for Thiers to bring his army to a strength of 130,000 in a brief time.

For almost all of the time that it existed, the Paris Commune had to wage an unequal struggle for survival, which consumed the greater part of its strength. Thus there is even greater reason for surprise and admiration at what the Commune managed to accomplish along the lines of the social and political restructuring of society.

The proletariat of Paris convincingly demonstrated that it was capable of taking over leadership of the country and deciding questions of significance for the entire nation. In a brief period, and amidst the trying conditions of a civil war, the Communards enacted a series of measures in the interests of the broad masses of the working people. Some of the Commune's decrees pointed the way to future generations of proletarian revolutionaries transforming the existing order according to the principles of the liberation of labour. The main accomplishment of the Communards was the liquidation of the police and bureaucratic apparatus left over from the Second Empire and its replacement with bodies truly representing the people.

The workers of Paris set high examples of proletarian internationalism and anti-militarism. The history of the proletariat's class struggle records their faultless morality, humanity, and heroism.

The first workers' government lasted only seventy-two days. The Communards were unable to hold off the united forces of French and international reaction. Their leadership suffered from serious theoretical errors and from insufficient consistency in fighting against their enemies. The army of the Versailles government, aided by its great numerical superiority, the collaboration of German troops, and treachery, managed to break into Paris. The Communards put up a heroic resistance, which was particularly strong in the workers' quarters of the city. Some six hundred barricades were erected in the streets, and a number of public buildings were set afire in an attempt to halt the advance of the well armed Versailles army, but to no avail. The German command perfidiously let Thiers's troops through to the rear of the Communards. The final battles were joined. Two hundred Communards held off the enemy for two hours at the Père-Lachaise cemetery. Most of them died in battle; the rest were taken prisoner and shot. Now a bloodbath began. It had been planned in advance, and was carried out at the orders of Thiers himself and of the command of the Versailles army. All those who had weapons in their hands, who wore military boots, or who were dressed in the uniform of the National Guard were shot. People were killed for a fancied resemblance to any of the Commune's leaders, and for looking askance at the butchers or making an incautious remark about them. Anyone with an Italian or Polish name was executed, because many Poles and Italians had fought on the side of the Communards. Anyone with powder burns on his hands suffered the same fate. In the hospitals, the wounded and the doctors alike were put to death. The leaders of the Commune were hunted like animals. Only in June did the executions without trial cease; the great number of unburied corpses threatened the city with an epidemic. The court trials went on until 1877. All in all, Paris lost some 100,000 of its best sons and daughters; they were shot, condemned to hard labour, sentenced to exile, and compelled to emigrate.

II

The First International gave its support to the proletarian revolution in Paris from the very beginning. Sections of the International Working Men's Association in Europe and the USA led a movement of solidarity with the first working-class government in history. Numerous meetings in Germany and Belgium, Switzerland and Austria-Hungary, Britain and the USA, and the pages of worker' newspapers proclaimed sympathy with the cause of the Communards. The situation in Paris was discussed by the General Council of the International.

At the session held on the evening of March 28, 1871, Marx suggested that an address be issued to the people of Paris. This suggestion was accepted, and Marx was charged with carrying it out. On April 4, however, Engels, who spoke for Marx in his absence, declared that such an address would be inopportune in the existing conditions. The General Council agreed with this.

Evidently the lack of news from Paris and uncertainty about conditions there would have made it difficult to draw up such a document. Furthermore, the bourgeois and reactionary press had launched a powerful slander campaign against the Commune. One of the fabrications advanced most often was that the Communards were guided in their actions by the General Council of the First International in London, that the events in Paris were part of a far-flung conspiracy of the"Reds." In these circumstances, the appearance of an address to Parisians from the General Council might have played into the hands of the reactionaries.

At the General Council's session on April 18, Marx suggested that an address concerning the general direction of the struggle be distributed among the members of the International. By this time he knew that what he would write was to be a theoretical work generalising from the experience of the new stage in the working-class movement, rather than an address to the people of Paris.

Marx already had at his command a large body of facts about the revolution. He regularly noted everything about events in France that he found in the newspapers to which he had access—mostly British and French organs hostile to the Communards. It was only rarely that the Commune's own publications reached him. Usually they were intercepted by the Versailles forces. By May, Marx's notes filled a thick notebook. Almost all of this material was used in the address.

In the latter part of April and in May, Marx wrote the final version. For the modern reader, the drafts have an independent interest; they help us not only to understand the creative process behind Marx's thought, but also to see more deeply into some of the theses of the final version. In working on his drafts, Marx was not constrained by considerations of space, and many of the subjects were developed in more detail, examined and explained more fully. The strict limits on the volume of the address forced him to omit from the final version several theoretically important passages to be found in the drafts.

The last of the Commune's barricades fell on May 28, 1871. It was just two days later, on May 30, that Marx read the final version of the address entitled *The Civil War in France* to the General Council of the First International. The document was approved, and it was decided to publish it.

In the early days of June 1871, a slender pamphlet of thirty-five pages appeared in an edition of 1,000. This outstanding document of Marxist thought, written in lucid English, organically combined high revolutionary feeling and forceful polemic with precise theoretical analysis. In accordance with the task in hand, Marx divided *The Civil War in France* into four sections. The first is devoted to the immediate pre-history of the Paris Commune, beginning with the revolution of September 4, 1870, and to the characterisation of the principal enemies of revolutionary Paris. The second details the history of the counter-revolutionary conspiracy against the rebellious French capital and the consequent rising on March 18, 1871. The third section explains the class essence of the Paris Commune as a working-class government expressing the interests of the majority of the city's working people. Here Marx contrasts the Commune with bourgeois government, which had become a hindrance in the path of social progress. In the fourth and final section, he describes the reign of terror brought by the victory of reaction, pays due tribute to the heroism and selflessness of the Communards, and predicts certain victory for forces of the international proletariat in the battles to come. Marx begins his work with a characterisation of the Government of National Defence. He attributes its rise to power to the rapidity with which events in France developed. Some of the workers' most influential leaders were still in prison. The Prussians were quickly nearing the French capital. The representatives of the big money bourgeoisie were able to exploit the patriotic fervor of the Parisians in their own interests. It was not for the defence of the Motherland, however, that they wanted power. "Paris," wrote Marx, "was not to be defended without arming its working class... But Paris armed was the Revolution armed. A victory of Paris over the Prussian aggressor would have been a victory of the French workman over the French capitalist and his state parasites. In this conflict between national duty and class interest, the Governmemt of National Defence did not hesitate one moment to turn into a Government of National Defection."[12]

In his moral portrait of the bourgeois who had come to power, Marx points out the features typical of the bourgeoisie as a class that has become a hindrance in the path of social progress. He shows that Favre, Picard, Thiers, and their like had achieved wealth and influence by dishonest, and often criminal, means. He exposes the bourgeoisie's class egoism. For many of its representatives, the victory of the popular revolution meant not only the end of the prosperity they had achieved, but also a possibility of imprisonment. Those who came to power on September 4, 1870, were inspired with a fierce hatred for the proletariat of Paris by their fear of punishment for the crimes they had committed. They would stop at nothing to retain their predominant position. They betrayed the interests of their own nation, and entered into secret negotiations with the enemy. While publicly swearing to defend Paris, they were covertly preparing to capitulate. Concluding peace with Germany was the prelude to waging war against Paris. The exploiter classes of France were planning to place the main burden of the indemnity of five thousand million francs to be paid to Germany on the country's working people. The revolutionary masses were an obstacle to accomplishing this, and so disarming the rebellious French capital was, as Marx wrote, "the first condition of success.[13]

Because of the occupation of a considerable part of the country by German troops and the isolation of Paris from the provinces, the forces of reaction were able to win out in the elections to the National Assembly, the predominantly monarchist make-up of which created well-founded alarm for the future of the republic.

The Thiers government openly provoked the Parisians to an armed uprising. The city was deprived, in practice, of its status as France's capital; the National Assembly pointedly withdrew to Versailles. Republican newspapers were forbidden. Two of the revolutionary leaders most popular among the city's working people, Blanqui and Flourens, were sentenced *in absentia* to death. The postponement of payment on promissary notes and for rent, which had been granted to the inhabitants of Paris during the siege, was revoked. Thousands of tradesmen and small shop owners were threatened with ruin. Many working people were faced with the real possibility of being turned out into the streets together with their families

The reactionaries directed their main thrust against the National Guard of Paris, which was made up mainly of workers. Three hundred thousand armed proletarians, with powerful artillery in their possession, were seen as a grave danger by the French bourgeoisie, and disarming them was the chief objective in the struggle against revolutionary Paris. The Thiers government was preparing for the decisive battle. Former Bonapartist generals were appointed to key posts in the city administration: governor of the city, prefect of police, and commander-in-chief of the National Guard. Troops loyal to the government were brought into Paris.

In the face of the threat of a counter-revolution, the National Guard closed its ranks and perfected its organisation. The conflict came to a head on March 18, when the government tried to seize the National Guard's artillery. Marx clearly shows the falsity of the pretext Thiers offered to justify his action. The Prime Minister asserted that the cannon of the National Guard were government property, when in actual fact, as Marx points out, they had been bought with money collected from the working people of Paris.

The night attack by government troops, Marx writes, marked the actual beginning of the civil war. The events of March 18 ended in victory for the people. "The glorious working men's Revolution...took undisputed sway of Paris. The Central Committee was its provisional government."

Marx calls attention to the fact that the proletariat came to power almost without bloodshed, in striking contrast to the revolutions, and especially the counter-revolutions, of the "better classes."[14] He shows up the lying fabrications of the bourgeois press, which had sought to frighten the common man with tales of bloody horror about the Paris revolution. Marx showed that the shooting of generals Lecomte and Thomas was a spontaneous expression of the masses' indignation; they were killed by government soldiers who had gone over to the rebels. Marx argues that there was also good reason for the breaking up of the demonstration of Parisian reactionaries by National Guards in Place Vendome. He proves irrefutably that it was not a peaceful procession of civilians, but a provocatory sortie by an armed class enemy. During the disturbance two National Guardsmen were killed, and ten more were gravely wounded. When the enemies of the revolution were put to flight, Marx writes, they left "the whole scene of their exploit strewn with revolvers, daggers, and sword-cases, in evidence of the 'unarmed' character of their 'pacific' demonstration."

Marx's address points to the sharp contrast between the humanitarian behaviour of the Communards and the savagery of the bourgeoisie. It cites instances, taken from newspaper accounts, of the ruthless punishment meted out to Communards who fell into the hands of the Versailles forces. Marx brings his readers to the thought that the killing of prisoners without trial or investigation (and the abhorrent sufferings often inflicted on them beforehand) is no exception, but rather the rule for the defenders of the bourgeois order. The Communards' desire to avoid taking life unnecessarily, Marx writes bitterly, and their unwillingness to unleash a civil war, ultimately proved to be a tragic error. He says in his address that "the Central Committee made itself...guilty of a decisive mistake in not at once marching upon Versailles, then completely helpless, and thus putting an end to the conspiracies of Thiers and his Rurals."[15] Equally ruinous were the inconsistencies of the Commune's leadership in conducting terror against the counterrevolutionaries. As Marx shows, the Commune's decrees on hostages initially had a sobering effect on Thiers and his generals. This decree said that anyone caught in complicity with the Versailles government was to be taken hostage, and that three hostages would be executed for every Communard put to death by the enemy. For a time no more prisoners were shot in Versailles. But when it was perceived that the Communards were slow in carrying out the terrible threats of their decree, the mass killings of Paris's captured defenders were resumed. Marx expresses particular disgust at the way that the Versailles rulers and their press gloated over these atrocities.

In the third section of the address, Marx gives a class analysis of the Commune. Many people of that time (including both friends and enemies of the Communards) could see that the March 18 revolution was accomplished by the hands of the workers of Paris. Some were even able to perceive the social essence of the Commune's main goals. And it was no secret to the vanguard of the European proletariat or to the most insightful members of the exploiter classes that the working people of Paris were fighting not only to preserve the republican form of government, but also to create a republic that would provide conditions for the freeing of labour from exploitation.

Almost no one, however, was able to indicate precisely what was fundamentally new, the thing that the Paris Commune, as the prototype of a future government of the victorious proletariat, manifested in embryonic form. For some, the election of the Commune was a natural reaction against the over-centralisation of Louis Bonaparte's police and bureaucratic government apparatus. For others, it was an echo of the turbulent times of the great bourgeois revolution in France at the end of the eighteenth century. For still others, it almost seemed a rebirth of the struggle waged by the communes of medieval towns for their freedoms and privileges.

It was no easy matter to find the truth amidst this multiplicity of views, especially seeing that the Communards themselves did not always have a clear idea of the direction and significance of their actions. Many of their slogans and proclamations were capable of obscuring matters still further. "It is generally the fate of completely new historical creations," Marx wrote, "to be mistaken for the counterpart of older and even defunct forms of social life, to which they may bear a certain likeness."[16]

In the days when the Paris Commune was not yet a matter for the history books, when the streets of the French capital were still strewn with its defenders and the ruins were still smouldering, it was only the perspicacity of genius that could see the proletarian republic just destroyed as a new page in world history, the first herald of a future society of working people.

The point of departure Marx takes for his analysis of the essence of the Paris Commune is a conclusion he arrived at nearly twenty years before the proletarian revolution in Paris. In one of his most important works, *The Eighteenth Brumaire of Louis Bonaparte,* Marx writes that the proletariat cannot fundamentally restructure society simply by making use of the government machinery it inherits from the exploiter classes. It must destroy that machinery and create something fundamentally new to replace it. What would the victorious working class set up in place of the bourgeois government apparatus? It was the Paris Commune that supplied Marx with the answer to this question.

The analysis of bourgeois government and the outline of its history presented in *The Civil War in France* is a brilliant example of materialist dialectics. Marx shows that "the centralised State power, with its ubiquitous organs of standing army, police, bureaucracy, clergy, and judicature",[17] came into being as a weapon of the newly emerged bourgeois society in its struggle with feudalism. Thus he admits that the rise and development of the bourgeois state was—objectively speaking—of a progressive character. But the contradictoriness of capitalism as a society of exploitation did not fail to make itself felt here too. The power of the state, "which nascent middle-class society had commenced to elaborate as a means of its own emancipation from feudalism ... full-grown bourgeois society finally transformed into a means for the enslavement of labour by capital." The Second Empire of Louis Bonaparte represented "the most prostituted and the ultimate form of the State power." Marx defined in a single phrase the class essence of that regime, which had pretended to represent the interests of nearly all segments of society. "In reality," he wrote, "it was the only form of government possible at a time when the bourgeoisie had already lost, and the working class had not yet acquired, the faculty of ruling the nation."[18]

"The direct antithesis to the Empire was the Commune."[19] What did Marx see that was fundamentally new in the organisation and activity of the municipality of Paris elected by the working people of the city through universal suffrage? First of all, that the majority of the Commune's members were either workers or acknowledged representatives of the proletariat. Marx saw another crucial difference between the new order in Paris and the bourgeois government in the organisation of the Commune's work and in the rights and obligations defined for its members. The Commune did away with the division of legislative and executive power typical of bourgeois parlia-

mentarianism, a system that the exploiter classes of capitalist society continue to this day to use for the maximum concealment of the class character
of their state. Representative democracy is thus used as a screen to mask the
continued existence of a well-regulated and potent government machine, the
purpose of which is to defend the interests of the powers that be. The first
working-class government, which had appeared in Paris, "was to be a
working, not a parliamentary body, executive and legislative at the same
time."[20] The Parisians had the right at any moment to demand an account
from the representatives they sent to the Commune, and even to recall those
who did not justify the trust placed in them by the people. Even today, the
members of a bourgeois parliament retain their mandate until the next
elections, whether they continue to have the support of the electorate or not.
All those who served the new proletarian order, including the members of
the government, were paid as skilled workmen; government service was no
longer a lucrative sinecure for members of the privileged classes.

Together with the meretricious bourgeois democracy, the victorious proletariat did away with the two main supports of the old regime: the standing
army and the police. Marx explained that the replacement of the standing
army by the armed masses of the people was dictated by the concrete
historical conditions that had come into being on the eve of the March 18
revolution. The victory won by the working people of Paris on that day was
in large measure due to the inability of the Thiers government to put sufficient troops in the field against the National Guard of Paris, which included
virtually all of the city's inhabitants who were capable of bearing arms. The
indisputable superiority of the armed masses was further strengthened by the
Commune's decree abolishing the standing army. The demand that such
armies be done away with was very popular in the working-class and socialist movement at that time. The proletariat rightly saw bourgeois armies as a
force intended to preserve the existing order. It was only the bitter experience of the class struggle (including the tragic fate suffered by the Paris
Commune) that made it clear to workers that the armed resistance of the
exploiters can be overcome with only the help of a well-organized regular
army. But in such cases a standing army is not in opposition to the people,
but rather defends its interests.

To destroy the machinery of the material power exercised by the
exploiter classes, it was also necessary to abolish the conditions that enslaved
the working people spiritually. Marx hailed the Commune's decree separating
church and state, and gave special importance to the liberation of education
from the influence of the clergy.

The measures the Commune took to abolish the instruments that kept the
masses politically and spiritually enslaved were not the invention of its
members. Many general-democratic programmes had called for an end to

bourgeois bureaucracy and standing armies, to police forces and the domination of the churchmen; the First International also stood for these goals. It was only after the proletariat of Paris had made these slogans a reality, though, that it became evident what was really at stake: the dismantling of the whole mechanism of the bourgeois state and the attainment of a fundamentally new level of democracy, described by Lenin as directly linked to "overstepping the boundaries of bourgeois society and beginning its socialist reorganisation."[21] It was in this that Marx saw the true social character of the Paris Commune. "It was...," he wrote, "a working-class government, the product of the struggle of the producing against the appropriating class, the political form at last discovered under which to work out the economical emancipation of Labour."

Marx understood full well that in the midst of a civil war, surrounded by enemies, the Commune could do no more in the social sphere than adopt measures meant to "betoken the tendency of a government of the people by the people." Among the decrees Marx considered as manifesting a socialist direction were the abolition of night shifts in bakeries, the prohibition of arbitrary fines and deductions from workers' pay, and preparations for turning enterprises abandoned by their owners over to workers' associations.[23] While not overvaluing the significance of these steps towards the socialist restructuring of society, Marx perceived that the common element uniting them was their overt anti-capitalism. "The Commune," he wrote, "intended to abolish that class-property which makes the labour of the many the wealth of the few. It aimed at the expropriation of the expropriators by transforming the means of production, land and capital, now chiefly the means of enslaving and exploiting labour, into mere instruments of free and associated labour.[24]

Marx thought it of enormous significance that the Commune was the first revolution "in which the working class was openly acknowledged as the only class capable of social initiative."[25] *The Civil War in France* presents convincing proof that broad segments of the petty bourgeoisie of Paris, and even of the middle bourgeoisie, acknowledged the proletariat's leadership in the revolution. Speaking before the General Council of the First International on April 25, 1871, Marx called the Commune's adoption of measures furthering the interests of these class groups a truly masterly move.

With a deep faith in the good sense of the proletariat, Marx noted that the workers who had come to power possessed no "ready-made utopias to introduce *par décret du peuple.*" Here Marx is alluding fairly openly to the behaviour of certain anarchist leaders, in particular Bakunin, during the revolutionary actions in Lyons in September of 1870. Instead of organising the workers to defend the power that had fallen into their hands, the anarchist leaders had composed a dismaying appeal that decreed the abolition of government. The time lost thereby hastened the downfall of the Lyons revolution. The working class, Marx wrote, is aware "that in order to work out their own emancipation, and along with it that higher form to which present society is irresistibly tending by its own economical agencies, they will have to pass through long struggles, through a series of historic processes, transforming circumstances and men."[26]

Marx's work showed the ways by which the proletarian revolution could be spread throughout France. Of course he knew quite well that the Parisians' chances of victory were insignificant, but an analysis of the potential that lay in the Commune was requisite for working out the strategy and tactics to be used by the proletariat in future struggles.

Marx argued that if the rest of the country followed the example of Paris, the Commune could become the organisational nucleus for the entire administrative system of France. He was confident that the dominance of the working class could be ensured in large industrial cities through electing communal self-governments, and hoped that in a little while the urban proletariat would be able to induce producers in rural areas to follow its lead.[27] It was his opinion that the workers' government had at its disposal all the means to accomplish this: it could free the peasantry from paying the indemnity of five thousand million francs to the Prussians that the French ruling classes had burdened it with, and from conscription. The power of the proletariat would have freed them from "the tyranny of the *garde champêtre,* the gendarme, and the prefect; would have put enlightenment by the schoolmaster in place of stultification by the priest." Most important of all, it was only a government of workers that could solve in favour of the peasantry the question of mortgage debt—that is, could liquidate or at least reduce the debts owed to banks and usurers, which hung heavily over small and middlesized peasant allotments.[28]

This was the answer that the address gave to the question of the proletariat's allies in the revolution, one of the keystones of Marxist theory.

Marx paid special attention to the Commune's internationalism. He saw in the first proletarian revolution an organic unity of the national and the international "Within sight of the Prussia army," he wrote, "that had annexed to Germany two French provinces, the Commune annexed to France the working people all over the world." For Marx, the internationalism of the Paris revolution was a natural expression of its proletarian character, a striking contrast to the nationalism and chauvinism of bourgeois society. He saw the internationalist essence of the Commune embodied in the appointment of Leo Frankel, a German (or, more precisely, Hungarian) worker, as minister of labour, and of representatives of the Polish revolutionary movement as commanders at some of the main points in the city's defences. "The Commune," he noted, "admitted all foreigners to the honour of dying for an immortal cause.''

The Civil War in France names the decree on the toppling of the Vendome Column, a monument to Napoleon's wars of conquest, as proof that the
Commune had opened a new era in the history of international relations.[29]

For Marx, Paris in the hands of its workers represented the exact opposite, morally speaking, of the old society. The proletarian government proved
to be the least costly in the history of France. As for the Communards'
caution in regard to bourgeois property, Marx thought that it had actually
gone too far. The Commune's stringency towards its civil servants was in
sharp contrast to the festering corruption of the Second Empire and the
Versailles government. The change wrought in the French capital by the
flight of the big capitalists, the bureaucrats, and the parasites associated with
them was truly astonishing. ''No more corpses at the morgue,'' Marx wrote,
''no nocturnal burglaries, scarcely any robberies; in fact, for the first time
since the days of February, 1848, the streets of Paris were safe, and that
without any police of any kind.''

Preoccupied with the prospects of building a new and just society, the
Parisians, regrettably, underestimated the forces of the old world that
opposed them. ''Paris,'' Marx wrote bitterly, was ''almost forgetful ... of the
cannibals at its gates.''[30]

All the segments and factions of the exploiter classes, laying aside their
old quarrels, joined to oppose the first workers' republic. The French bourgeoisie and the ruling elite of the German empire, which not long before had
faced one another on the battlefield, were quick to reach an understanding.
Marx stressed again and again that without Bismarck's help Thiers would
have been wholly unable to put together the army he needed to crush the
proletarian revolution in Paris. The armed forces of the Versailles government were largely made up of prisoners of war from the old Bonapartist
armies, handed over by the German command. The underhanded role played
by Prussia's ruling circles was not confined to this. ''Whenever before,''
Marx asked irately, ''has history exhibited the spectacle of a conqueror
crowning his victory by turning into, not only the gendarme, but the hired
bravo of the conquered government?'' The perfidy of the German high
command was particularly unseemly in view of the fact that Prussia had
formally declared its neutrality, and Bismarck offered countless assurances to
the European public that German troops would not interfere in France's civil
war. The concerted attack on the Commune by all the forces of reaction in
Europe made it possible for Marx to arrive at a conclusion of enormous
importance for the development of the proletariat's revolutionary theory.
''Class-rule is no longer able to disguise itself in a national uniform; the
national governments are *one* as against the proletariat.''[31]

Thiers had been able to keep the rebellious French capital from uniting with the movement in the provinces, and Marx saw this as one of the reasons for the downfall of revolutionary Paris. Thiers had stopped at nothing to achieve his purpose. The policies of the Versailles government had combined deceit, cynical lies, and intrigues with savage repression of revolutionary stirrings in the rest of France.

The selfless heroism and nobility of the defenders of Paris emerge from the pages of *The Civil War in France* in striking contrast to the sadism of the enraged bourgeoisie. Marx compares the behaviour of the Versailles government's soldiers to the bloody orgies of the darkest times in the history of ancient Rome. Here is what he sees: "The same wholesale slaughter in cold blood; the same disregard, in massacre, of age and sex; the same system of torturing prisoners; the same proscriptions, but this time of a whole class; the same savage hunt after concealed leaders, lest one might escape; the same denunciations of political and private enemies; the same indifference for the butchery of entire strangers to the feud. There is but this difference, that the Romans had no *mitrailleuses* for the despatch, in the lump, of the proscribed, and that they had not "the law in their hands' nor on their lips the cry of "civilisation'." The vengeance inflicted *en masse* on the vanquished was especially repellent against the background of the frenzy of the bourgeois elite in Paris.

In counterdistinction to the saviours of capitalist society, who had lost all semblance of humanity, the working people of Paris offered an example of self-sacrifice "unequalled in any battle known to history."[32] Marx's work exposed the attempts of the exploiter classes to hide their crimes behind a thick curtain of lies and slander. Here was an example of what could be expected from capitalism: "In all its bloody triumphs over the self-sacrificing champions of a new and better society, that nefarious civilisation, based upon the enslavement of labour, drowns the moans of its victims in a hue-and-cry of calumny, reverberated by a world-wide echo."

In those days, all of the bourgeois and reactionary press was full of malicious and absurd fabrications about the reign of anarchy, murder, and arson that Paris had supposedly suffered under the Communards. The greatest outcry among the hired quill-drivers was provoked by the setting of fires as a means of defending the Commune and by the execution, in the last days of the fighting in May, of a number of hostages—priests, policemen, and gendarmes.

Marx defended unconditionally the right of the Communards to regard fire as a weapon in the struggle against the superior forces of the enemy. He presented irrefutable examples showing that the bourgeoisie, while hypo-critically condemning the soldiers of the Commune for burning public buildings, had unscrupulously and needlessly consigned to the flames not only outstanding architectural monuments, but even whole towns. Marx emphasised especially that the same people who were lamenting the destruction of a few palaces and mansions had looked on complacently on the wholesale massacre of captives after the battle.[33]

Marx's address proved beyond the shadow of a doubt that it was not the Communards, but rather the Versailles government, that was actually responsible for the execution of the hostages. He shows that it was only in answer to the bourgeoisie's brutal practice of shooting war prisoners that the Commune had seized hostages.

By continuing their mass executions of captured Communards, the government forces provoked the defenders of Paris into taking retaliatory measures. The Commune repeatedly offered to give up Darboy, the archbishop of Paris, and the other priests among its hostages in exchange for Blanqui, who had fallen into the hands of the Versailles government. Marx argued that it was Thiers, who persisted in rejecting these offers, that was the real murderer of the archbishop.[34]

International reaction, which had closed ranks in the face of the first proletarian revolution, launched a furious slander campaign against the First International, which was represented to the horrified man in the street, as Marx says, "in the manner of secret conspiracy, its central body ordering, from time to time, explosions in different countries."[35]

One of the main lessons for the international proletariat to be drawn from the Commune was the realisation that there can be no reconciling the interests of the exploiters and the exploited. "After Whit-Sunday, 1871, there can be neither peace nor truce possible between the working men of France and the appropriators of their produce," Marx states in his address. He had no doubt about who would ultimately be the victor: "...The French working class," Marx wrote, "is only the advanced guard of the modern proletariat."[36]

The concluding lines of the address are a requiem for the heroic Communards, and an angry condemnation of their butchers. With the foresight of genius, Marx predicted that "working men's Paris, with its Commune, will be for ever celebrated as the glorious harbinger of a new society. Its martyrs are enshrined in the great heart of the working class. Its exterminators history has already nailed to that eternal pillory from which all the prayers of their priests will not avail to redeem them."[37]

The General Council of the First International outlined an extensive programme of measures to popularise the address on *The Civil War in France*. Particular importance was given to distributing it among the proletariat. The price of the pamphlet (sixpence) was reduced by half for members of working-class organisations.

There was a need to keep the bourgeois press from using one of its favourite weapons—silence—against the General Council's address. It was decided that copies should be sent to trade union councils, to the editorial offices of several liberal newspapers, and to leading figures in each of the two principal parties in the British parliament. The newspapers of the ruling classes soon understood that they would be unable to keep this document of the International Working Men's Association in obscurity. Respected London papers such as *The Times,* the *Telegraph,* and *The Standard* devoted editorials to *The Civil War in France*. They had to acknowledge, albeit through clenched teeth, the "excellent literary style" of Marx's work.[38] Of course, the bourgeois papers furiously assailed the ideas and views promulgated and defended in the address. In the grim atmosphere that hung over Europe after the Paris Commune, the militantly revolutionary tone of *The Civil War in France* and its uncompromising expressions acted on the bourgeoisie in the way a red cloth acts on a bull. Marx wrote to one of his acquaintances: "It is making the devil of a noise and I have the honour to be at this moment the best calumniated and the most menaced man of London."[39]

Marx participated actively in the newspaper polemics that sprang up around his work. He saw them as a fine opportunity to explain and defend the ideas of the Paris Commune and of the International to the European public at large.

Some of the organs of the bourgeois press tried to call into doubt the address's portrayal of those who had been most brutal and hypocritical in suppressing the Commune, men like Thiers, Favre, Picard, and Ferry. They made their charges against the General Council of the International Working Men's Association, in whose name *The Civil War in France* had been published. In his reply, Marx publicly acknowledged that it was he who had written the pamphlet which was causing such a furore and recommended that his opponents bring suit against him for slander.[40] He had absolute confidence that no bourgeois newspaper would be able to overturn his scathing assessment of the leading figures in the Versailles government.

By the end of June the first English-language edition of *The Civil War in*

France was completely sold out. The General Council decided to put out a second edition of 2,000 copies and to lower the price to twopence. In suggesting that this be done, Marx again stressed the need to circulate the address widely among workers.

Translations of *The Civil War in France* were of great importance in its popularisation. All of the International's organisations, from the General Council to the local sections, took an active part in this work.

Marx and Engels paid close attention to the preparation of the translations of *The Civil War in France*. Their desire was that each translation reflect not only the original text, but also the specific traits of the working-class movement in the country into whose language it was rendered. This is why some of the translations edited by Marx and Engels depart on occasion from the original. Engels played a very large part in circulating and popularising the address. He not only edited translations of it, but also supervised its delivery to the appropriate presses, gave advice on the manner of its publication and the size of the printing, carried on an extensive correspondence on these questions with leaders of the working-class movement, and publicised the address in proletarian newspapers.

During 1871 and 1872, the address was translated into French, German, Russian, Spanish, Polish, Italian, Danish, Flemish, and Dutch. The first publications of *The Civil War in France* to appear outside England were issued by the working-class press. Marx and Engels placed particular importance on the appearance of the German version. At that time the Social-Democratic Party of Germany and the German proletariat were the vanguard of the whole European working-class movement, exerting a perceptible influence on its development in other countries. For this reason Marx and Engels regarded bringing one of the fundamental documents of scientific revolutionary theory to the attention of the foremost representatives of the German working class as a top priority task. Engels was in direct communication with the editors of *Der Volksstaat*, the central organ of the German Social-Democrats. He also did the work of translating. Engels's translation was sent in instalments to Wilhelm Liebknecht, the paper's editor, who was one of the leaders of the German Social-Democrats and a personal friend of his and Marx's. After the address had appeared in *Der Volksstaat*, the manuscript of the translation was sent off once again, this time to Switzerland, where it was printed in the magazine *Der Vorbote*, one of the popular organs of the International. By the autumn of 1872, some 11,000 copies of *The Civil War in France* were in print in Germany. Working-class newspapers brought out special impressions. Marx's work not only circulated all through the proletarian press of Europe, but also crossed the Atlantic. Lengthy excerpts from it appeared in American newspapers, and selections were read at a meeting of sections of the International Working Men's Association held in New York in July of 1871.

The Civil War in France left no one indifferent. It evoked a wide range of feelings, from profound admiration to burning hatred. "I have received the address and read it," one of the leading figures in the International wrote to Engels. "It is superbly written." Professor E. S. Beesly, a noted British scholar and bourgeois radical-democrat, called the appearance of *The Civil War in France* the most important event of the year.[41]

Police agents turned their attention to the address. In a report to the prefect of the Paris police, an informer in Brussels wrote that *The Civil War in France* had been read at a meeting in the headquarters building of the Belgian section of the International. There is no denying that the author of the report had certain powers of understanding. The main purpose of the address, he said, was to explain and justify the actions of the International and particularly of the Paris Commune. The agent called his chief's special attention to Marx's characterisation of the Commune as a government of the working class, a product of the struggle between the producing class and the expropriating class, and so on.[42]

The years to come saw the appearance of new editions of *The Civil War in France* in various languages.

The ideas formulated in the address marked a new step in the development of Marxist theory. It was after the Paris Commune that Marx and Engels gave their teaching on the dictatorship of the proletariat its final form. In numerous works, published over more than twenty years, they had been working towards this conception, which is one of the most important in Marxism. In the Commune, Marx and Engels saw the real embodiment of a dictatorship of the proletariat. Marx did not actually use the term in *The Civil War in France*. He called the Commune "a working-class government." Two months later, however, in a speech on the seventh anniversary of the International given at a special meeting in London, he not only emphasised again that the Commune had embodied "the conquest of the political power of the working classes", but drew from the experience of the Communards a conclusion of far-ranging theoretical importance. He indicated that dictatorship of the proletariat is a necessary condition for the total liquidation of all forms of exploitation.[43]

There were many reasons why it was imperative to develop, clarify, and popularise the ideas presented in *The Civil War in France*. Even many of Marx's comrades in arms were unable to fully grasp the theoretical depth of his work. The enemies of Marxism within the working-class movement (above all the anarchists) tried in every way possible to distort the essence of the address and to weaken its influence on the proletarian masses as far as they were able. The followers of Bakunin vehemently denied the need for a dictatorship of the working class in a socialist revolution. They tried to show that Marx's work was inconsistent, that he had lost his way among its contradictions. According to the anarchists, the author of *The Civil War in France* was not sincere in his support for the Communards, which was dictated by his fear of losing his popularity among workers. It was even claimed that Marx had been compelled by such fears to amend some of his fundamental views.

The opportunists who had sprung up within the workers' movement were also frightened by the experience of the Paris Commune. The last third of the nineteenth century was a relatively peaceful period in the development of the proletariat's class struggle. Working-class parties emerged and grew strong in the countries of Europe. In some (Germany, for instance) they became a real social and political force. Social-Democrats now sat in the supreme legislative bodies of a number of capitalist countries. Given these conditions, there were a good many leaders in the European working-class movement who felt disinclined to remember the heroic experience of the Parisian workers and the conclusions Marx had drawn from it. More and more often, they sought to represent the Commune as an example of weak organisation, theoretical immaturity, and the ruinous consequences of pursuing unrealistic goals.

Marx and Engels, in their struggle against these opportunist trends within the working-class movement, persistently instilled the main ideas of *The Civil War in France* into the consciousness of the proletariat's vanguard members. There was a need to help workers understand that the dictatorship of the proletariat was necessary stage on the way to the revolutionary transformation of society. Engels wrote about this in his well-known work *The Housing Question* (1872): He argued that "*every* real proletarian party ... has put forward ... the dictatorship of the proletariat as the immediate aim of the struggle".[44] Ignoring this immutable truth, Engels thought, would lead to a break with the working-class movement and a rapprochement with petty-bourgeois socialism. Three years later, Marx returned to this idea in his critique of the programme of the German Social-Democrats adopted at the unification congress in Gotha. This document made serious concessions to opportunist views about the development and goals of the working-class movement. Exposing the falsity of hopes that a socialist society could be created within the framework of a bourgeois republic (even if the latter were democratic), Marx wrote: "Between capitalist and communist society lies the period of the revolutionary transformation of the one into the other. Corresponding to this is also a political transition period in which the state can be nothing but the *revolutionary dictatorship of the proletariat.*"[45] This, one of the main theses of Marxist theory, is a direct development of the conclusions drawn in *The Civil War in France*.

In 1891, on the occasion of the twentieth anniversary of the proclamation of the Paris Commune, a third, commemorative edition of the German version of Marx's work appeared. It included an introduction written by Engels. At a time when the working-class movement was rapidly gathering strength, when the Social-Democratic parties of the developed European countries were winning more and more supporters in the parliamentary elections, Engels thought it opportune to call the attention of his proletarian audience once again to this work by Marx, which he called "half-forgotten".[46] Recalling the content of the address of the General Council, Engels supplemented it in several highly important ways. In essence, what he did was to further develop certain of Marx's ideas, making them more concrete and precise by putting them into historical perspective. He gave a brief characterisation of the chief groups represented in the Commune, the Blanquists and the Proudhonists. The first, he said, were "at that time Socialists only by revolutionary, proletarian instinct" The thinking of the second was based on the mistaken and utopian notions of the petty-bourgeois socialist Proudhon. It was reality, however, the practice of revolution, that guided their actions. Engels writes that "in both cases the irony of history willed ... that both did the opposite of what the doctrines of their school prescribed."[47] This remark is of exceptional importance for the understanding of the organic connection between the Paris Commune and Marxism, of the genuine admiration for the Communards that is evident in *The Civil War in France*. Most of the Commune's leaders had not read Marx and did not share his ideas. But the inescapable logic of the class struggle prompted them to take actions that Marx, guided by his genius, had foretold in many of his works. All attempts to turn aside from the tactical line set out in Marxist theory ended in utter failure and brought nothing but harm to the Communards. This was why the Commune marked the end of several non-Marxist trends within the French working-class movement (and not there alone). Engels develops Marx's idea that the old machinery of government must be broken in the course of a proletarian revolution and stresses that this applies to all forms of exploitative state, including the bourgeois democratic republic. Citing the USA as an example, Engels characterised the class essence of America's much vaunted democracy with astounding accuracy. "...We find here," he wrote, "two great gangs of political speculators, who alternately take possession of the state power and exploit it by the most corrupt means and for the most corrupt ends." Engels, in his introduction, far-sightedly warned German workers against "a superstitious reverence for the state and everything connected with it."[48] He further stated that "in reality... the state is nothing but a machine for the oppression of one class by another, and indeed in the democratic republic no less than in the monarchy."[49] In unmasking the falsity of bourgeois democracy, Engels was not at all setting up an opposition between the dictatorship of the proletariat and the organisation of power in democratic forms. In a work written three months after his introduction to *The Civil War in France*, he called the democratic republic "the specific form for the dictatorship of the proletariat."[50]

Engels, writing at a time when opportunism was becoming more and more perceptible within the working-class movement, concluded his introduction to *The Civil War in France* with these celebrated words: "Of late, the Social-Democratic philistine has once more been filled with wholesome terror at the words: Dictatorship of the Proletariat. Well and good, gentlemen, do you want to know what this dictatorship looks like? Look at the Paris Commune. That was the Dictatorship of the Proletariat."[51] This paragraph was aimed against those in the Social-Democratic movement who wanted to root out of the memory of the European working class the militant spirit of *The Civil War in France*.

Attempts to neutralise the revolutionary content of Marxism ended in utter failure. Lenin and his comrades-in-arms came to the defence of Marxist theory and continued its development under new historical conditions.

The Civil War in France occupies a special place among those works by Marx to which Lenin turned most often. Almost throughout his revolutionary career, Lenin carefully studied the conclusions drawn from the experience of the Paris Commune in the address of the General Council of the First International. As early as March of 1904, he used Marx's work in preparing for a lecture on the Paris Commune to be given at an international meeting of émigrés in Geneva.

The first Russian revolution in 1905-1907 sharpened still further Lenin's interest in the ideas formulated in *The Civil War in France*. In 1905, he made a fresh translation of it into Russian, giving the working-class movement in his own country a fitting rendering of one of the fundamental works of Marxism.

While yet another revolutionary crisis in Russia was taking shape, Lenin once again made a careful study of the address of the General Council. At the end of 1916, much of his attention was focussed on solving the problem of the state in Marxist theory. By the beginning of the February revolution of 1917, he had filled the famed "blue notebook" with extracts on this subject. *The Civil War in France* occupies a large place among this material. The outcome of this study was Lenin's brilliant work *The State and Revolution*. The seventh, final chapter, which Lenin had entitled "The Experience of the Russian Revolutions of 1905 and 1907", remained unfinished. "I was 'interrupted' by a political crisis," he wrote. Lenin was not disappointed by this experience, however. "It is more pleasant and useful to go through the 'experience of the revolution' than to write about it," he noted in his afterword to the first edition of *The State and Revolution*.[52]

Lenin highly esteemed *The Civil War in France*. He called it a work which *"to this very day* serves as the best guide in the fight for 'heaven' and

as a frightful bugbear to the liberal and radical 'swine'.''[53] Between the two
Russian revolutions of 1917, the February and the October, Lenin returned
to the address for the solution of three fundamental problems. First, there
was the need to recover from oblivion and bring before the workers the fruits
of Marx's genius. Lenin wrote that ''now one has to engage in excavations,
as it were, in order to bring undistorted Marxism to the knowledge of the
mass of the people. The conclusions drawn from the observation of the last
great revolution which Marx lived through were forgotten just when the time
for the next great proletarian revolutions had arrived.''[54] Lenin understood
full well that it was not only, or even mostly, time that had helped to erase
one of the fundamental works of Marxist theory from the memory of the
proletariat. To a significant extent, this state of affairs had been brought
about intentionally by those who were not happy with the revolutionary
conclusions Marx had drawn in his work. Lenin held that the changes in
public and political life since 1871 were characterised by rapid growth of
bureaucratism (''bureaucracy has everywhere soared'', as he put it). He saw
the greatest danger in Social-Democratic parties infected with opportunism
which had been ''by 3/4 grown into a *similar* bureaucracy.''[55] ''Under
capitalism,'' he wrote, ''democracy is restricted, cramped, curtailed, muti-
lated by all the conditions of wage slavery, and the poverty and misery of the
people. This ... is the reason why the functionaries of our political organisations and trade unions are corrupted ... by the conditions of capitalism and
betray a tendency to become bureaucrats, i.e., privileged persons divorced
from the people and standing *above* the people.'' The main difference
between the reformists and the revolutionaries, Lenin thought, was that the
former sought to improve the bureaucratic machinery of the state, while the
task of the latter was to destroy it.[56] It is easy to understand why the
reformist leaders of the Social-Democrats were not the least bit inclined to
remind the working class of Marx's idea that the bourgeois state machine
must be destroyed, a dictatorship of the proletariat established, and so on.
Lenin regarded the fight against the opportunists, who attempted to shore up
their distortions of Marxist theory with quotations from Marx, as a task of
primary importance. ''The experience of the Commune,'' he wrote, ''has
been not only ignored, but distorted. Far from inculcating in the workers'
minds the idea that the time is nearing when they must act to smash the old
state machine, replace it by a new one, and in this way make their political
rule the foundation for the socialist reorganisation of society, they have
actually preached to the masses the very opposite and have depicted the
''conquest of power' in a way that has left thousands of loopholes for
opportunism.''[57] In *The State and Revolution,* Lenin subjected to withering
criticism the distortion and vulgarisation by Bernstein and Kautsky, leading
figures in the Social-Democratic Party of Germany, of the ideas Marx had

expressed in *The Civil War in France*. He clearly revealed the ill intent of Bernstein's attempts to identify Marx's view of the lessons of the Commune with the views of Proudhon, one of the founders of anarchism. Bernstein had claimed that "as far as its political content is concerned", Marx's programme for organising state power on a communal basis "displays, in all its essential features, the greatest similarity to the federalism of Proudhon" This kind of shuffling disgusted Lenin, but did not surprise him. "...It is no accident," he wrote, "for it never occurs to the opportunist that Marx does not speak here at all about federalism opposed to centralism, but about smashing the old bourgeois state machine which exists in all bourgeois countries."[58] Lenin drew a precise line between the views of the Marxists about the state and the Commune and those of the anarchists. "The former," he wrote, "recognise that after the proletariat has won political power it must completely destroy the old state machine and replace it by a new one consisting of an organisation of the armed workers, after the type of the Commune. The latter ... deny that the revolutionary proletariat should use the state power, they reject its revolutionary dictatorship."[59] Lenin used Kautsky as an example of how a Marxist could degenerate into an opportunist. One of the chief indicators of the change was Kautsky's rejection of the revolutionary conclusions Marx drew from the experience of the Paris Commune.

Lenin's book did more than defend the fundamentals of Marxist theory from attempts to revise them. Lenin used Marx's analysis of the Commune as an aid in working out a strategy for the working class in the approaching proletarian revolution in Russia. Like Marx, who had uncovered in the Commune a political form by which it would be possible to bring about the economic liberation of labour, Lenin uncovered in the Soviets the nucleus of the future power of the working people. He pointed out the internal similarities between the Commune and the Soviets. The government of the Parisian proletariat and the bodies created by Russian workers at the time of the revolution of 1905-1907 had much in common. They were the result of the creativity of the masses, which had risen up to overthrow the old order, and embodied their desire to do away with the oppressive machinery of the exploiter classes. Both the Commune and the Soviets of Workers' Deputies marked the first steps in creating a new, proletarian type of state. "...The Russian revolutions of 1905 and 1917," Lenin wrote, "in different circumstances and under different conditions, continue the work of the Commune and confirm Marx's brilliant historical analysis."[60]

Lenin returned over and over again to the ideas of *The Civil War in France* even after the victory of the October Revolution. Polemicising against Kautsky, who had once and for all gone over to the counter-revolutionaries, Lenin accused him of falsifying Marxist theory. Using *The Civil War in France* as a point of departure, Kautsky tried to depict Marx as an adherent of "pure" democracy, and to place the concepts of dictatorship and democracy, in opposition to one another, ignoring their class essence.

The war of ideas over Marx's outstanding work still goes on today. It intensified after the *Civil War in France* was accorded a place of honour in the theoretical arsenal of the victorious Russian proletariat and its Party. In the 1920s, the opportunists expended no little effort trying to reduce its significance, to make of it no more than yet another of the numerous sources for our understanding of a bygone time. They argued that the address of the General Council had been written in the heat of a fierce fight by an open supporter of one of the two sides, and thus could not claim to be dispassionate and merited no more than critical study.

Bourgeois ideologues continue their furious attacks on the understanding of the Paris Commune that has grown up in Marxist-Leninist theory. The claim that it is based on a "myth of the Commune", among sources of which *The Civil War in France* is named. It is argued that that Marx's main motive in creating this myth was to usurp the inheritance of the Communards and use their popularity among workers for his own selfish interests. The enemies of Marxism try to show that the picture of the Paris Commune that emerges from the address of the General Council of the First International is not in accordance with reality. Modern critics of Marx think that the Paris Commune was not actually a proletarian revolution and did not show a socialist slant. And in no way, they say, can it be regarded as a prototype of the dictatorship of the proletariat. All of that was supposedly invented by Marx, and then seized upon and elaborated by his supporters and followers. Those who make such claims often resort to out-and-out falsifications to support them.

The fierceness of the polemics that continue to rage around *The Civil War in France* shows yet again how important Marx's work is, even today. Efforts continue to be made to neutralise the revolutionary essence of Marxism-Leninism, and the address of the General Council continues to play an important role in the fight to keep it pure, reminding the working class of the imperishable value of the fundamental theses of Marxist theory.

Marx's work continues to have great significance as a model of the creative development of that theory, of its enrichment with the experience of the proletariat's class struggle.

The Civil War in France asserts the necessity of proletarian internationalism as an inalienable quality of socialist revolution and condition for its success. What is meant here is the practical manifestation of internationalism and its role in defending a real, existing government of workers.

The address of the General Council teaches the proletariat the importance of creating a militant proletarian organisation to act as the vanguard of revolution, and shows the significance of the working class's alliance with other segments of the working population.

Marx's work retains a special topicality for those segments of the pro-letariat and proletarian parties that must wage their struggle under a military or fascist dictatorship or a police and bureaucratic regime that limits bourgeois-democratic freedoms. Many passages in *The Civil War in France* seem to be addressed directly to such groups within the international revo-lutionary and working-class movement. They are reminders of the hard lessons that the Paris Commune has to teach: that the success of revolution depends on the readiness of society and the proletariat's level of develop-ment, that the combined forces of international reaction opposing it repre-sent a grave danger, that revolution must be able to defend itself, that a ruthless struggle must be waged against counter-revolution, in which inde-cision and hesitation are fatal errors.

At the same time, the address of the General Council strengthens the desire of the proletariat to "storm the heavens", and shows an example of a scientific, class-based approach to the people's revolutionary movement. It fosters in the working-class party an ability to correctly assess the character and prospects of any given proletarian action, a readiness to lead it or to come to its aid not only in the hope of immediate success but also in the long-term interests of the whole revolutionary struggle of the working class. What is more, Marx teaches that in certain cases one can and should risk temporary setbacks, in the face of which courage and organisation must be preserved.

The Civil War in France will live in the memory of the working class as an eternal monument to the Communards, who first laid siege to capitalist society, and as an example of the power, vitality, and currency of genuinely scientific revolutionary thought.

1. Lenin, *Collected Works* 21: 143
2. Lenin, *State and Revolution*, p. 42; NY 1943
Note: page numbers standing alone refer to pages in this book.
3. p. 24
4. p. 25
5. p. 27
6. p. 28
7. p. 31
8. p. 33
9. p. 34
10. p. 9
11. p. 34
12. pp. 36-7
13. p. 45
14. p. 48
15. p. 51
16. p. 59
17. p. 54
18. p. 56
19. p. 56
20. p. 57
21. *State and Revolution*, p. 83
22. p.60
23. p. 65
24. p. 61
25. p. 62
26. p. 61
27. p. 58
28. pp. 63-4
29. p. 65
30. pp. 67-8
31. p. 80
32. p. 75
33. pp. 76-7
34. p. 78
35. p. 81
36. pp. 80-81
37. pp. 81-82
38. Marx-Engels, *On the Paris Commune*, p. 252, Moscow, 1976
39. *Letters to Dr. Kugelmann by Karl Marx*, Moscow-Leningrad, 1934
40. M-E, *Paris Commune*, p. 248
41. *Pervy Inernatsional i Parizhskaya Kommuna*, (The 1st International and the Paris Commune), p. 522, Moscow, 1977 (in Russian)
42. Ibid., p. 372
43. Marx-Engels *Collected Works 22:* p. 634
44. M-E *CW 23:* p. 372
45. *Critique of the Gotha Programme*, p. 18, NY, 1966
46. p. 10 (this book)
47. p. 18
48. pp. 20-21
49. p. 22
50. Engels, "Critique of the Draft Social-Democratic Programme of 1891," M-E *Selected Works 3:* p. 435, Moscow, 1977
51. p. 22 (this book)
52. *State and Revolution*, p. 101
53. Lenin, *C.W. 12:* 111
54. *State and Revolution*, p. 97
55. Lenin, *Marxism on the State*, p. 50, Moscow, 1977
56. *State and Revolution*, pp. 96-7
57. Ibid., 100
58. Ibid., pp. 45-6
59. Ibid., pp. 94-5
60. Ibid., p. 48